AROUND THE TUBE IN 80 PUBS

by
Mike Gerrard & Pete Gerrard

Around the Tube in 80 Pubs

By
Mike Gerrard and Pete Gerrard

PUBLISHED BY
80 Guides Publishing
England

Cover illustration of The Southampton Arms in Kentish Town Copyright (c) secretartistnw5, website: www.secretartistnw5.com

Book formatting & design by TJ Wiltshire, website: www.tjwiltshire.com

All photos copyright (c) Pete Gerrard unless otherwise credited.

TABLE OF CONTENTS

THE PUBS BY TUBE STATIONS IN ALPHABETICAL ORDER

INTRODUCTION

Let's make it clear. We are not saying that these are the eighty best pubs in London. They are certainly eighty of the best, but for inclusion in this book there was one main criterion, apart from the quality of the pub itself. Each one had to be, at the most, a 10-minute walk from a tube station.

This is not because we don't like walking. We have done, between us, classic walks like England's Pennine Way and the Samaria Gorge on Crete. But we thought a guide to pubs near tube stations might appeal to visitors to London, as well as to Londoners themselves. In fact, Londoners might appreciate the proximity to a tube station when leaving one of these pubs rather than when going to it.

In addition to being close to a tube station, we did have other requirements. The pubs had to be ones that we wanted to return to. Good beer is, of course, taken for granted. That's why you'll find included here some of the relatively new pubs, like some in the BrewDog chain, alongside bigger outfits like Fuller's and Nicholson's. Just because you belong to a multi-million pound corporate conglomerate doesn't mean that the individual landlord concerned doesn't keep a good pub selling well-kept beer.

We looked for other qualities too. A few hundred years of history certainly helped. Pubs with a riverside or canalside setting was another plus. So if you want a pub with a River Thames or London canal view that's only a 10-minute walk from a tube station, this is definitely the book for you.

We also looked for pubs at mainline stations, as everyone knows what it's like to wait for a train, and what better way is there to kill some time than by enjoying a nice beer? That's why you'll find delights like Euston Tap and Waterloo Tap in our selection. That's also why one of our 80 pubs isn't even a pub. It's The Sourced Market at St Pancras International, but you can buy a beer there and consume it on the premises, in an enjoyable setting, so in it goes.

The idea for the book came about when we were meeting friends from the USA who were visiting London. We took them to The George in Southwark, and they were bowled over by it. Well, who wouldn't be? It was a part of London they'd never have gone to if we hadn't suggested it. After a couple of excellent pints, we then showed them how to use the tube to get back to their hotel. They'd been daunted by it and up till then had walked everywhere. Hmm, we thought. There must be other people like this, who want the experience of visiting a good London pub, but don't know where to start.

The Blackbird, famous for its pies.

We ourselves started with a short list of about ninety pubs that were close to a tube station, with the aim of whittling it down to eighty. They were mostly pubs we already knew, some from many visits over the years, but we also included some recommended by others, and some we'd always been meaning to visit but hadn't got round to.

Then began the noble task of visiting all ninety – even the ones we visited regularly anyway - to decide if they were good enough to include in our guide. A few fell by the wayside, for various reasons, like the beer or the atmosphere, or the attitude of the staff. And no, we weren't asking for a free pint. We should stress that every pint we had in every pub in this book was paid for by ourselves. And we never mentioned we were researching a book. We visited all ninety as ordinary pub-goers, and some more than once.

Eventually we whittled the list down to the magic eighty that you can read about in the following pages, although a few are on the waiting list for Volume Two. What – another eighty good pubs all within ten minutes of a tube station? Well, at a rough estimate the city has about 7,000 pubs so we might just manage it.

If you want to see all the pubs on one map, it looks something like this:

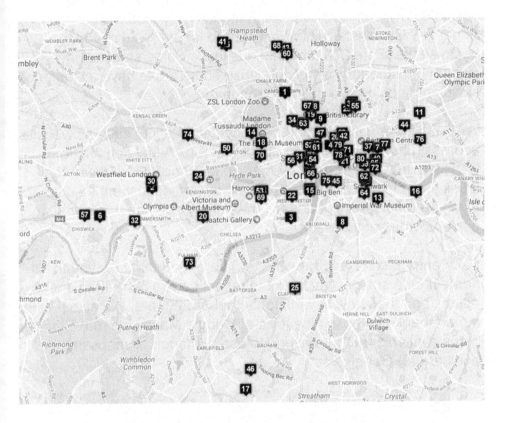

You can see this map online at https://tinyurl.com/80Pubs

HOW TO USE THIS GUIDE

We've tried to make the guide as simple and as user-friendly as possible. The pubs are listed alphabetically by tube station, from Angel to Westminster. There isn't a pub for every tube station, because there are 270 tube stations in all. Some stations have several pubs nearby, simply because some areas have a wealth of excellent pubs, like Angel and Monument.

With each pub you'll find the Practical Information, such as website, address, phone number and opening hours. A few don't have websites, and one doesn't even have a phone. We've given the times they serve food, if they do, but just because there's no times given for food serving it doesn't mean they don't do it, just that they don't provide set times.

Each entry begins with How to Get There, and that tells you the nearest tube station, which exit to take if there's more than one option, and then how to walk to the pub from there. We also provide a map thanks to those nice folks at Google Maps who make their maps available free for anyone to use, although all maps in this book are (c) Google.

The Blackfriar

If you have a smartphone you can try using the Google Maps app, and while we've found it mostly accurate there are one or two places where we have, well, fallen out with it.

We then follow with a bit of Local Information. This picks out what you might see on your way to the pub, or what attractions are nearby if you have time for a short detour.

Finally there's a description of the pub, letting you know the atmosphere to expect, nice places to sit, and beers you might expect to find there. We haven't attempted to give a definitive list of the beers available, as of course these do change from time to time. Many of the best places have guest ales too, which constantly change. All we can do is tell you what we had to drink on our visits, and some of the beers that are reasonably regular favourites. This is a guide to pubs near tube stations, and it's safe to say that in every pub in this book you will enjoy a decent pint of something. Or two.

USING THE LONDON UNDERGROUND

As we mentioned in the Introduction, this book was in part inspired by being able to help friends visiting London to master the tube system. It's not complicated, when you get used to the way it works, and compared to somewhere like New York it's a piece of cake.

What's in a Name?
Most Londoners call it the tube, and it's also called the underground. Just don't refer to it as the subway. A subway is a pedestrian tunnel that goes under the street, or one that takes you out of the tube station and under the street to the other side.

The Lines
The tube network, as symbolised by its iconic map, is made up of a number of lines. Master the map and the lines and you've mastered getting around.

Each of its 11 lines interconnects and each is indicated by a different colour. The Central line, for example, is red, and the Circle line is yellow. Look at the tube map and the colours help you distinguish the lines, and see where they connect if you need to change lines. Most journeys only require one change, at the most, with a few needing two. If you need to change more than twice, then you've got a complicated journey.

Lines run north-south or east-west, even if they don't run exactly in those directions. Anyone who's driven in the USA will be familiar with that. You can be on a southbound train even if you're actually heading west at various stages. It's the overall principal that matters.

The Tube Map
You should definitely get a pocket tube map when visiting London, although all stations will have large tube maps on the walls somewhere. They aren't always easy to get to, though, if there's a crowd of people so always carry your own. Pick up a free map at any tube station, or download one to your smartphone.

The map was designed in 1931 and became a classic for the way it simplifies the tube network and makes it easy to follow. The main thing to beware of is that it is not to scale and not a reflection of the way the city is on the surface, Two stops that might appear to be unconnected on the map might turn out to be close together above ground, so if you're not familiar with the city always use the tube map in conjunction with a street map, the London A-Z being the most common and best.

Also, just because one station is where two lines meet, it doesn't mean it's only a short distance from one line to the other one. In some cases, like Monument and Bank, they appear to connect on the map but it's a long walk from one to the other. Above ground the stations are five minutes apart.

Spooky
In one of those spooky coincidences of modern life, at the exact moment those words were being typed an email arrived from Transport for London letting us know that they have devised new maps which show how long it takes to walk from one tube station to another. You can find out everything you want to know about using the tube, and the Docklands Light Railway and other transport systems, including buses, on the Transport for London website. It also has a very helpful Journey Planner: https://tfl. gov.uk.

The Docklands Light Railway
The DLR was opened in 1987 as a way of extending the public transport network into the docklands area of east London, mainly to serve Canary Wharf and other financial headquarters, as well as the huge Excel conference centre. You can use your Oyster card on the DLR network. Four of its stations are underground, and many of its stations link with the tube system, but the DLR is a light metro system and is not the tube. For that reason, we've excluded it from this book even though it will take you to many delightful pubs. Something for us for the future, perhaps?

Using the Tube

If you're not familiar with the tube network, begin your journey by consulting your map. If you don't yet have one, check the large-scale maps that are in every tube station ticket office and on every platform.

The trains themselves only contain a map of the line you're on, though there are several of these in every carriage. The maps will show you which stations connect with which other lines, and announcements before you come into a station will also give you this information.

Before setting off, you need to work out the best way to get from Station A, where you are, to Station B, where you're going. That might sound simplistic to people who use the tube every day, but it needs stressing for the benefit of confused city visitors.

If there isn't a direct route try to figure out the route with the fewest changes. Then memorise the route. 'Take the Piccadilly line going west towards Heathrow or Ealing. Get off at Leicester Square and change to the Northern line going southbound towards Morden.'

It's important to remember the end destination as well as the line you want, as that's what will be displayed on the front of the train and on the overhead information board on each platform. The board will tell you the next few trains that are due, and how long till each one arrives.

Some tube lines divide and different trains will go to the different end destinations. Also, not all trains will go to the very end of the line. Note that if it matters which train you get, we tell you in the directions for each pub. If it doesn't matter, just get on the first train.

And always remember, if you make a mistake you just turn round and go back. The vast majority of people on the tube are regular users and can probably tell you what you need to do without even thinking about it.

Oyster Cards

The easiest way to get round on the tube is to use an Oyster card. This is a plastic card like a credit card which you can top up online or at any station. Oyster cards automatically work out the cheapest available way for you to get around, and cap the daily payment you make.

Provided you have credit, you simply touch it on the electronic readers at every barrier and they then open to let you into or out of the tube. A few stations don't have barriers so you must look for the Oyster card machine and validate your card otherwise you might get charged too much.

It costs £5 to get an Oyster card, and this is refundable if you surrender the card, as is the unused balance on the card.

Other Options

There are many other options for buying tickets, but the best one
for you will depend on your personal circumstances so it's beyond
the scope of this book to recommend the best choice. You can buy,
for example, a 7-day travelcard. This would be cheaper if you use
it on all seven days, but if you don't use it every day then an Oyster
card might still be cheaper.

In the Zone

The tube network is divided into nine zones, and fares are
calculated according to how many zones you travel through. Zones 1
and 2 are in the centre of London, and it may be you only travel
within those zones. A 7-day travelcard that covers all nine zones is
almost three times as much as one that only covers Zones 1 and 2.
If you're buying a travelcard you have to work out in advance which
zones you're going to be travelling in, and that is not always
possible, of course. That's another reason why the Oyster card is
usually the best choice. We believe in keeping life simple and as
cheap as possible. It leaves more money to spend on beer.

Cask Marque

On some of the pub photos you'll notice a Cask Marque logo, like this:

Cask Marque is an independent non-profit making organisation
which runs an accreditation scheme to promote pubs serving great
quality cask ale. 10,000 licensees hold the award and their beer
is checked a minimum of twice a year when all cask ales on sale
are tested for temperature, appearance, aroma and taste. All beers
must pass to gain or retain the award. Onsite training is provided
where necessary to ensure the consumer is guaranteed a great
pint, every time.

AROUND THE TUBE IN 80 PUBS

THE CHARLES LAMB PUB AND KITCHEN

HOW TO GET THERE

Angel tube station on the Northern line is only a short walk away from the Charles Lamb, and it's on the Bank section of the line when it splits in two as it works its way through London. If you're on the platform and the overhead displays are only showing tubes going via the Charing Cross branch, travel to either Euston in the north or Kennington if coming from the south, and change there.

When you step out on to the pavement from the tube station, you should turn left and start walking down Islington High Street until you reach the junction with Pentonville Road. It will only take you a minute to get there. Turn left here, and stay on the left, because the road will fork soon and you'll need to take the left hand branch of the fork. Soon after the fork turn left into Colebrooke Row and then turn right down Elia Street, a short way along Colebrooke Row. The Charles Lamb soon comes into view, on the corner of Elia Street and Quick Street.

LOCAL INFORMATION

The Angel doesn't have too many heavenly connections, but it is linked to land belonging to St John's Priory, because it was on their land that The Angel Inn was first recorded in 1614. Continuing to trade over the centuries, the Inn still had fields to the south of it as late as the early 1800s, when the land was built on and London became one vast sprawl from the centre of the city out to Islington.

The Angel stopped being a pub in 1921, and the ground floor now belongs to the Co-Operative Bank. You'll see it on the way to the pub, on the corner of Islington High Street and Pentonville Road. There is still an Angel pub here, and you'll pass it as you walk down Islington High Street, but it's not on the original site. It's a Wetherspoons pub, and is fairly typical of that ilk.

As we've pointed out elsewhere, there are several pubs in the area that are mentioned in this book. The others are The Narrowboat, The Earl of Essex, and the Duke of Cambridge, and they are close enough together to get around in one pleasant ambling session.

16 Elia St, London N1 8DE
Open: Mon-Tue 4–11pm, Wed-Fri noon-11pm,
Sat 11am-11pm, Sun noon-10.30pm
Tel: 020 7837 5040
www.thecharleslambpub.com

DESCRIPTION

The Charles Lamb Pub and Kitchen is a cosy little pub liberally decorated with hops dotted about the place, and it benefits from being slightly off the beaten track. Incidentally, if you're coming from the Earl Of Essex pub, you walk down Danbury Street and cross over the canal, take an immediate right at the little roundabout into a continuation of Danbury Street, and then a second left down Quick Street.

It doesn't have the largest selection of ales in the world, but there are usually four to choose from. Dark Star's Hophead lived up to its reputation on our last visit.

And who was Charles Lamb? He was a writer in the 18th and early 19th centuries, a contemporary of Coleridge and Wordsworth, and amongst many other titles he produced a book in 1823 called 'Essays of Elia', which remains perhaps his most famous work. The street that the pub stands on was named Elia Street (the book came before the street, and indeed the pub, which opened in 1839). It wasn't till 2005 that the pub was named after the author.

THE DUKE OF CAMBRIDGE

HOW TO GET THERE

Your nearest station for the Duke of Cambridge, or to give it its full name The Riverford at The Duke of Cambridge (all will be revealed later), is Angel, on the Bank stretch of the Northern line and one stop away in either direction from King's Cross and Old Street. When you leave the station, head towards the right hand side of the main exit and walk off to the right along Islington High Street. Shortly after passing Charles Place you'll see the rather striking statue of Hugh Myddelton, who was largely responsible for keeping great parts of London supplied with fresh drinking water from the start of the 17th century.

Mr. Myddelton's statue marks the entrance to Islington Green, and you should now turn right and walk down the road that bears the same name. Islington Green ends just before a turning off to the right comes into view, and this is called St. Peter's Street. Turn into St. Peter's Street and walk along it for a short way until you reach a junction with Danbury Street and Rheidol Terrace. The pub will be in front of you, where St. Peter's Street and Danbury Street meet up.

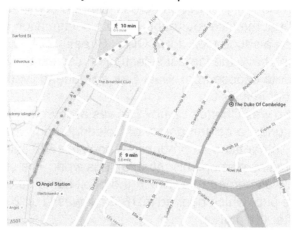

LOCAL INFORMATION

Islington Green is just across the road from The Screen on the Green, a single-screen cinema dating back to 1913. It looks like the top half of an old-fashioned Wurlitzer jukebox.

The Green itself is a triangle of common land that has somehow managed to evade developers over the years, and now allows for a pleasant little stroll if you're killing a few minutes before heading for the pub.

There are quite a few pubs in this area, and four of them are mentioned in this book, which made for a very pleasant Sunday evening when we were last here. The others are The Narrowboat, The Earl of Essex, and The Charles Lamb.

30 St Peter's St, London N1 8JT
Open: Mon-Sat noon-11pm, Sun noon-10.30pm
Food: Mon-Sat noon-4pm, 6.30pm-10.30pm,
Sun 12.30pm-4pm, 6.30pm-10pm
Tel: 020 7359 3066
http://dukeorganic.co.uk

DESCRIPTION

As mentioned earlier, the full name of this pub is The Riverford at The Duke of Cambridge, which Google sums up as an 'organic pub with stripped-wood décor'. That's a nice way of saying that you're somewhere that may well remind you of an old school classroom, with benches to match. Large unadorned windows and a plain wooden floor give it an airy feel.

Our first beer here was an interesting one, from Dominion Brewery, who used to be known as Pitfield. It was a Whisky Ginger Beer, or a ginger beer aged in whisky casks. Not much whisky flavour to it, but plenty of ginger, and the whole drink was nicely herbal and spicy.

The place is largely food-led and proudly organic, and there are usually four cask ales to choose from, with plenty of other alcoholic beverages to sample. And the name? The Duke of Cambridge was founded by Geetie Singh in 1998, and she later married Guy Watson, who hails from Riverford Farm and runs the Riverford Food Kitchen in Devon and, now, The Riverford Food Kitchen in the Duke of Cambridge. So now you know.

THE EARL OF ESSEX

HOW TO GET THERE

The closest tube stop for The Earl of Essex is Angel, on the Bank branch of the Northern line, although you may well reach it after visiting one of the three other pubs in the area that are described in this book. They are The Narrowboat, The Duke of Cambridge, and The Charles Lamb.

To get to Angel tube station you can easily catch a Northern line service that travels via Euston in the north or Kennington in the south, as Angel is only served by the Northern line. It's also one stop away from King's Cross, if that's more convenient for you.

You'll need to turn right on leaving the station, and head along Islington High Street until you reach a pub called The York. Turn right here, down Duncan Street, until you reach a T-junction with Colebrooke Row. Turn left here, with Colebrooke Row Gardens on your left, and then you'll need to take the second right. This is called Gerrard Street (hurrah!), and you walk down here until you meet Danbury Street. Turn left, and the pub is on your left.

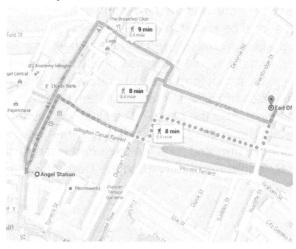

LOCAL INFORMATION

It would be interesting to watch a documentary that filmed this area from the air over the last four centuries, and took us forward in time to the present day with each century lasting for a minute. Impossible, obviously, but we can glean much from historical records.

This was mostly open land in the 17th century, apart from a few main roads. As the 18th century progresses, more lanes and footpaths are added, but there was still only one known building standing outside the centre of the town (as it was then) at the start of that century. It was, typically, an inn.

Cottages, brewhouses and inns were added as the century wore on, and in the 19th century we see houses that are three storeys high, floor-cloth factories, cattle markets, terraced houses, along with other wonders of the age. We were pleased to see Gerrard Street appearing in 1841.

The two World Wars inevitably took their toll on the area in the 20th century, but improvement works by the GLC in building flats and houses, along with plenty of council renovations from the 1960s onwards, helped the fabric of the area to recover.

25 Danbury St, London N1 8LE
Open: Mon-Thu noon-11.30pm, Fri-Sat noon-midnight,
Sun noon-11pm
Food: Sun-Tue noon-9pm, Wed-Sat noon-10pm
Tel: 020 7424 5828
www.earlofessex.net

DESCRIPTION

They no longer call them brewhouses but The Earl of Essex is that modern delight, the brewpub. At the time of writing there were thirteen keg lines and five cask lines, including two of their own. They're all displayed on a large board high up on the left wall as you enter.

The pub looks nice and bright from the outside, with a few potted shrubs and some good tile work. Inside, check the design behind the bar, which is pleasingly elaborate at the top with the rest of it being full of interesting bottles in front of a large mirror.

Before you settle down, take the chance to walk around the bar to the back of the pub. Apart from admiring the excellent illustrations on the walls as you go, and gathering a bit more space if it's getting busy at the front, you'll find out where their own beer comes from. You can even go out into the garden, if it's warm enough. We had an Oz Bomb from Arbor Ales on a recent visit, a crisp and refreshing golden ale that brightened up a rainy night in Islington. It says much for the pub that the rain wasn't keeping anybody away.

THE NARROWBOAT PUB

Photo courtesy of The Narrowboat Pub

HOW TO GET THERE

The Narrowboat Pub, as you might imagine from its name, is by the side of a canal, and Angel tube station is not too far away. It's on the Bank branch of the Northern line and just a short hop from the likes of Euston, Camden Town and London Bridge.

When you reach the main exit, head for the right-hand side of the station and turn right to walk past the front of the Royal Bank of Scotland. Turn right by the side of The York pub and proceed down Duncan Street. When you reach a T-junction turn left into Colebrooke Row and then almost immediately right into Noel Road.

Noel Road doesn't quite run in a straight line. When you reach Danbury Street, you'll need to make a little zig to the left and then a zag to the right to carry on with Noel Road until it reaches a roundabout. Turn right down St. Peter's Street and the pub turns up on your left on the corner of Baldwin Terrace just before you reach the canal.

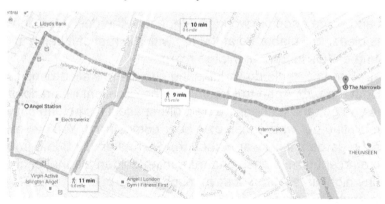

LOCAL INFORMATION

The canal that flows silently by the side of the pub is called Regent's Canal, and it's the Islington branch of it. First opened in 1820, it has a couple of nearby basins (City Road, Wenlock) that are fun to explore. Indeed, it is Wenlock Basin that is more or less opposite the pub.

Incidentally, when you walk down Duncan Street and turn into Colebrooke Row, the canal is in front of you almost hidden away behind a fence and a lot of shrubbery, although there is a small open gateway leading down to it. The canal disappears at this point into the Islington Tunnel, which is almost 900 meters long (2950 feet) and finally emerges not far from King's Cross Station.

If you're a fan of canals, then you might appreciate a trip to the London Canal Museum, which is a short walk to the west of Angel tube station and situated on New Wharf Road.

119 St Peter's St, London N1 8PZ
Open: Mon-Tue 11am - 11pm, Wed-Sat 11am-midnight, Sun 11-11
Food: Mon-Sat 11am-10pm, Sun 11am-9pm
Tel: 020 7400 6003
http://thenarrowboatpub.com

DESCRIPTION

The Narrowboat is one of a number of pubs in the area that are included in this book, and there's a very pleasant stroll to be had taking in The Duke of Cambridge, The Earl of Essex and The Charles Lamb as well as calling in here.

The pub is run by Young's, although the beer selection is by no means limited to their beers alone, and there are usually three guests on to whet the appetite. Beer can be consumed inside the pub but, weather and crowds permitting, you can always venture outside and watch the canal rolling by.

The interior has a fairly modern feel about it, even if some of the comfortable chairs are very difficult to remove yourself from. You just sink in and think: 'Well, that's us done for the next hour.' Whilst sipping away at our beers (Young's Special), one question was answered for us. Yes, people do still drink Spritzers. We thought they'd died out with Del-Boy and Only Fools and Horses (British television comedy, for overseas visitors), but they're alive and well in The Narrowboat.

THE BARLEY MOW

HOW TO GET THERE

Baker Street was one of the original underground stations when the network started operating in 1863. It's served by a number of tube lines - Circle, Hammersmith and City, Metropolitan, Bakerloo and Jubilee – and so it's easy to get to from most parts of the city. It's also a very confusing station, because of its sheer size. You need to find the Baker Street South exit and proceed to street level. If you turned right you'd be heading towards 221b Baker Street and the Sherlock Holmes Museum, but for now turn left towards Marylebone Road.

Before crossing over, it's worth taking a few paces to your left to stand in front of the Marylebone Road exit from the station, because here you'll find a statue of Sherlock Holmes himself.

To get to the pub, retrace your steps back to Baker Street, and turn left to cross over Maryle-bone Road. Do wait for the lights to change before crossing over. The pub's been there since 1790, so there's no need to rush.

When you've safely crossed over the road, carry on walking south down Baker Street until you reach Dorset Street on your left. Turn along Dorset Street and The Barley Mow is right there.

LOCAL INFORMATION

If we trace our steps back to the Sherlock Holmes statue, continuing east along Marylebone Road at this point would bring you to the Planetarium and Madame Tussauds, giving you the chance to be a fully-fledged tourist.

If you fancy a bit of an explore, Regent's Park is not too far away, and is home to the world famous Zoo as well as a boating lake, an open-air theatre and lots of lovely walks. Plan in advance and you might also get in a day's cricket at Lord's, which is a walk of about 20 minutes.

8 Dorset St, London W1U 6QW
Open: Mon-Sat noon-11pm, Sun noon-10.30pm
Tel: 020 7487 4773
www.chrishuey.co.uk/barleymow

DESCRIPTION

The Barley Mow is one of the most popular pub names in Britain, and is usually thought to refer to a sheaf of barley, one of the key ingredients of beer. The traditional folk song 'The Barley Mow' came later, being first noted in the 19th century, but the pub is of 18th century origin.

And while we can't promise that you'll find a pint of Red Kite from Vale Brewery when you get here (a nice pint of red, hoppy ale when we sampled it), we can promise you a place that the Campaign For Real Ale describe as 'an historic pub interior of national importance'. Good beer, too, with usually six ales to choose from.

It first gained its place as a Grade II listed building in July 2000, and it is richly deserved, as the interior of the pub is especially worth exploring, although the outside is also not without interest. Most striking inside are the two wooden drinking boxes that are attached to the wall and stand by the counter on the left. These are very small areas where people could go and drink when they wanted some privacy, a factor that was of great importance to the Victorians in particular.

There are plenty of other examples of Victorian handiwork to be seen around the place, and some fine prints of 18th-century Marylebone, so if you're like us you'll buy a pint and start wandering around, having a good look everywhere. If you're lucky, you might even find an empty drinking box.

THE ANGEL

HOW TO GET THERE

You'll be on the Jubilee line for this one, because the nearest tube station is Bermondsey. This sits just south of the River Thames between Canada Water and London Bridge stations, giving you plenty of connections via the Northern line to London Bridge and then a quick change to the Jubilee line.There's only one exit at Bermondsey station, and it will bring you out on Jamaica Road. You'll need to turn right, and you'll also need to cross over the road at some point. There's a crossing just outside the station, which seems as good a place as any.

Walking along Jamaica Road will see you pass on your left Wilson Grove, Marigold Street and Cherry Garden Street, and then you'll arrive at West Street. Turn left down here, crossing over the road fairly early on, because you'll soon see Paradise Street on your right. Walk along Paradise Street for a short way until Cathay Street pops up on your left, and turn down Cathay Street and make the short journey to the pub, which will appear in front of you. Just remember to stop when you reach the pub. If you don't, you'll end up in the River Thames.

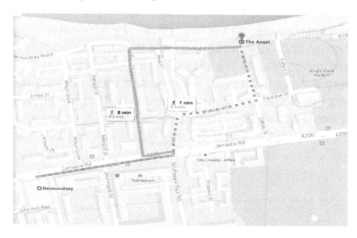

LOCAL INFORMATION

The Angel pub is run by Samuel Smith's brewery, and is one of a number of their pubs in London. Several of them are featured in this book, and they have various things in common. According to the Samuel Smith's website, all their pubs have these features:

- The architecture and fittings must be Victorian.
- Games, such as darts, are only played in the public bar.
- The pub does not have music or TV.

And that pretty much sums them up. They also sell only Samuel Smith's products, so don't expect to find Carling or Guinness in here. They produce their own beers, spirits, soft drinks and anything else that you could think of consuming. They even make their own crisps!

They're great ones for tradition, as befits the longest running brewery in Yorkshire (they were founded in 1758). At the brewery headquarters in Tadcaster, North Yorkshire, they've got their own shire horses, which are used to make local deliveries. You'll find them behind the Angel and White Horse pub, which is next to the brewery.

101 Bermondsey Wall E, London SE16 4NB
Open: Mon-Sat noon-11pm, Sun noon-10pm
Tel: 020 7394 3214
No website

DESCRIPTION

As the estate agents tell us, it's all about location, location, location, and this place has it in spades. What it doesn't have is cask beer, or at least it didn't have when we were last in. All the beers were dispensed on keg, so we settled on a couple of 4.5% stouts, which were excellent.

After a brief exploration of the various rooms downstairs we went up a few steps at the back of the pub so we could go outside and sit on chairs on a small balcony. The balcony doesn't just overlook the River Thames, it actually sits slightly above it. The tide was coming in when we were last there, and water was splashing up between the slats of wood beneath our feet. Much as we like the Thames, we had no intention of drinking any of it, in or out of our beers, so we moved to the opposite end of the balcony and sat down above calmer waters.

And what a view! If you want to stay away from the water you can always go upstairs and admire the scenery from inside, or stay downstairs and do the same, for that matter, but we love going out onto that balcony – and you will too.

THE KINGS ARMS

HOW TO GET THERE

You'll want the Central line for this one, because the nearest tube station to The Kings Arms is Bethnal Green. This gives you a good choice of starting points, as the Central line serves the likes of Oxford Circus, Tottenham Court Road, Liverpool Street and many more.

Leave the station by the Bethnal Green Road exit, and turn left to walk under a bridge that will be just in front of you. It's a case of keep going from now on, walking past Gales Gardens, Pott Street, Ainsley Street, Wilmot Street, Seabright Street and Viaduct Street, and then you'll reach Derbyshire Street on your left.

Walk down Derbyshire Street until you reach a park called Weavers Fields, and turn right without entering the park. Keep walking along Derbyshire Street with the park on your left, and when the park comes to a halt and the buildings begin, the Kings Arms will soon be on your left hand side. It does spell its name the Kings Arms, by the way, and not the King's Arms, so there.

LOCAL INFORMATION
Here's another bit of tube trivia to think about while you're waiting for your train to make its way along the Central line to Bethnal Green.

The Central line traces its origins back to 1900, when the first section of the line opened up. This ran from Shepherd's Bush to Bank, and the journey cost two old pennies. If you look at the map of the London Underground, you'll count 13 stations between Shepherd's Bush and Bank, but today the Central line serves a total of 49 stops, of which just 20 are actually underground. There were in fact 11 stations on the line when it first opened, as Bond Street narrowly missed the deadline and Holborn didn't come along until 1933. It ranges from West Ruislip in the west to Epping in the east, and if you count it in terms of total passenger journeys, it's the busiest line on the entire Underground network.

11a Buckfast St, London E2 6EY
Open: Mon-Thu noon-11.30pm, Fri-Sat noon-midnight,
Sun noon-11.30pm
Tel: 020 7729 2627
http://thekingsarmspub.com

DESCRIPTION
The Kings Arms was taken over and refurbished to its present format in 2013. The décor is fairly basic, functional rather than ornamental, but it works, and works well. If you're anything like us, your eyes will be drawn immediately to the impressive parade of fonts on the bar. There were 17 ales and 3 ciders to choose from when we were there, but you'll have to study the menu board on the wall to find out the details of what's on offer as none of the fonts have any information on them.

The last pint we had in here was Lord Marple from Thornbridge Brewery in Derbyshire, which aims to be nothing more than a session English bitter, and in this it succeeds admirably. As we said, it's fairly functional, wooden floor, small tables with wooden chairs and benches to sit on, and the walls are largely bare, with the exception of an interesting mounted moth and butterfly collection. Behind us was a large Blue Morpho (its wing-span is over six inches!), and there are many other beautiful specimens to examine, if that's your thing.

THE REDCHURCH BREWERY TAP

HOW TO GET THERE

It's all too easy to head off in the wrong direction with this one, as we did the first time, so let's take it carefully. First of all, you'll need to get to Bethnal Green underground station, which is on the Central line.

Leave the station using the exit for Bethnal Green Road, which brings you out at the junction of Bethnal Green Road and Cambridge Heath Road. When you reach ground level and have positioned the Salmon and Ball pub on your left (nice name), cross over the road towards Paradise Row then turn right and walk a handful of steps to the main road (Cambridge Heath Road), and head left.

You should now be walking past the splendidly named Paradise Gardens on the left, with Museum Gardens on the right across the road. Take a stroll around Museum Gardens, as it's not often that you'll find palm trees in London.

If not, just continue walking. Watch for a narrow street on the left called Poyser Street, just after The Dundee Arms. Turn down Poyser Street, follow it around to the right, and keep going until the Brewery Tap comes up on your right underneath a railway arch.

LOCAL INFORMATION

The Victoria and Albert Museum of Childhood is just north of Museum Gardens, and it was all about The Soup Dragon, Bagpuss, Noggin the Nog and The Clangers, when we went in. And if those names mean nothing to you, then that's a great shame. Don't let it put you off if they don't, as there are plenty of other things to enjoy.

If you were to remain on Paradise Row and later follow it around into Nant Street before joining Cambridge Heath Road and turning left, then Mother Kelly's bar on your left is worth a visit before you reach Nant Street, as it's got quite a range of draft and bottled beers. But let's be honest, there's not too much else to distract the casual visitor, so Redchurch Brewery Tap it is.

275-276 Poyser St, London E2 9RF
Open: Thu-Fri 6pm-12.30am, Sat noon-12.30am
Tel: 020 3487 0255
www.theredchurchbrewery.com

DESCRIPTION

When you enter the place you are literally inside the brewery. Before you get tempted to touch anything, head off to the left and go up the stairs to find the bar.

Shabby chic sums up the bar for us, looking like a slightly dishevelled but extremely comfortable, warm and friendly student common room that just happens to have a bar in it. The full range of Redchurch beers is highlighted, and there were a couple of interesting collaboration brews on our last visit, featuring the likes of De Molen and Hanging Bat.

The place is also a music venue at times, which is hinted at by the sight of the vinyl record player sitting opposite the bar. There's an eclectic sense of decoration about the place, and we couldn't resist asking about the hundreds of small drawings of cats that decorate the wall behind the bar. Apparently, like so many things, somebody with a little bit of time on their hands produced the initial drawing, and now it's all getting slightly out of hand.

There's a dart board near the top of the stairs, and if you fancy a game of darts do bear in mind that the bar is directly underneath train lines. You don't want to be aiming for double top when a London Overground service to Cambridge Heath rattles over your head.

THE BLACKFRIAR

HOW TO GET THERE

This extraordinary-looking building is just over Queen Victoria Street from Blackfriars underground station. The station is on both the Circle and the District lines, giving you plenty of choice about how to get there. It's also served by Blackfriars mainline train station and if you're feeling nautical, you can get here by boat to Blackfriars Pier.

To get to the pub after leaving the underground station, just cross over to the other side of Queen Victoria Street and you'll see it in front of you. You can't miss it; its shape always makes us think of a giant piece of cheese.

Before walking inside, however, stroll along a little way further down Queen Victoria Street, because you're just a short distance away from the wonderfully named Anglican church 'St. Andrew by the Wardrobe'. It was the last church that Wren designed for the city of London, although the present building is a complete reproduction as it was first destroyed in the Great Fire of London before being bombed out in the Blitz during the Second World War. And if you want to know why it's 'by the Wardrobe', you'll have to pay them a visit and pick up a leaflet from the foyer.

LOCAL INFORMATION

The Blackfriar is one of the Nicholson chain. The majority of these are in London, where the Nicholson brothers James and William first plied their trade as distillers of gin in the 19th century. They were based in both Clerkenwell and Bow, and the Bow site still stands, although there's been no distilling there since the end of the Second World War.

William Nicholson was the Chairman when the first pub opened in 1873. He was a major cricket enthusiast, and was good enough to play for Middlesex for over 20 years. In the space of 5 years in the 1860s, he gave almost £40,000 (a colossal sum at the time) to the MCC, which enabled them to buy the freehold to Lord's cricket ground and to build a new pavilion.

The Nicholsons supplied many pubs in the East End of London with their gin and if any landlords were unable to pay their bills, the company stepped in and bought their pubs. Their pub empire therefore expanded, and they also bought many so-called 'gin palaces', which tended to be architecturally splendid and marvellously ornate sites. One particular art nouveau site, remodelled in 1905 on the site of an earlier pub from 1875, is The Blackfriar.

174 Queen Victoria St, London EC4V 4EG
Open: Mon-Sat 9am-11pm, Sun noon-12.30am
Tel: 020 7236 5474
www.nicholsonspubs.co.uk/restaurants/london/
theblackfriarblackfriarslondon

DESCRIPTION

There may be a sign outside promoting Worthington Ales on Draught, with a thirsty friar downing some beer, but don't expect to find any. What you will find is a Grade II listed building, built on the site of a 13th-century Dominican priory. This explains why you can see friars dotted all around the pub in various sculptures and mosaics. We spotted one friar crawling along on his hands and knees, being helped by a colleague. If he was doing that in here, he'd be on a wooden floor, gazing up at the marble bar and the detailed friezes.

Assuming you're upright, of special interest is a dining area at the back of the pub, entered through one of three archways. Lined in marble and alabaster, and featuring some large mirrors, the walls have a number of intricate engravings. And don't forget to look up at the ceiling, it's marvellous. Despite appearances, this is a later addition to the pub.

While you enjoy your drink, reflect that we very nearly lost this architectural gem in the 1960s, as property developers were greedily eyeing it up. Thanks to the work of some tireless campaigners, including Sir John Betjeman, the pub was saved. We raise a toast to those campaigners every time we're here.

YE OLDE CHESHIRE CHEESE

HOW TO GET THERE

Blackfriars is the closest tube to Ye Olde Cheshire Cheese, and it's on the Circle and District lines.

When you come out of the tube station, turning left will take you to Blackfriars Bridge and a pleasant view out along the Thames. It will also take you to the wonderful Blackfriars pub, described elsewhere in this book. To get to Ye Olde Cheshire Cheese, though, you'll need to turn right, cross over Queen Victoria Street at the traffic lights and head north along New Bridge Street. Keep walking along New Bridge Street until it reaches a junction with Fleet Street. A pub called The Albion is just before the junction, on the left hand side.

Cross over Fleet Street so that you're on the northern side of it, and turn left, keeping an eye out for alleyways like Poppin's Court, Shoe Lane and Peterborough Court, which pops up twice. Shortly after its second appearance you'll see what resembles a square lantern hanging overhead, advertising the name of the pub. A walk down Wine Office Court to the right of the sign reveals a very different pub from that suggested by the frontage on Fleet Street.

LOCAL INFORMATION

Fleet Street has long been associated with printing and publishing, and it's been taking place here for over 500 years. The street is named after the River Fleet, which is now largely underground and flows from Hampstead into the River Thames, but there was plenty of it above ground until the end of the 19th century.

The Daily Courant was London's first daily newspaper, appearing in March 1702, and it was – of course – published on Fleet Street. More and more papers started appearing, and Fleet Street thrived alongside them until the majority of them left towards the end of the 20th century. Some publishers remain, and the free Metro newspaper is one of them, along with DC Thompson and their Beano comic featuring Dennis the Menace. There have been almost 4000 editions of The Beano published over the years, ever since it made its first appearance in 1938. Now that's a cause for celebration if ever we heard one, so let's celebrate with a drink in Ye Olde Cheshire Cheese.

145 Fleet St, London EC4A 2BU
Open: Mon-Fri 11am-11pm, Sat noon-11pm, Sun noon-4pm
Tel: 020 7353 6170
Website: None

DESCRIPTION

As the signs outside tell you, this pub was rebuilt in 1667 after the Great Fire of London, and on entering you could be forgiven for thinking that very little has changed since then. There's been a pub on the site since 1538.

It is part of the Samuel Smith's chain and like many of their establishments you have to see the interior to believe it. On multiple levels, with numerous rooms, it's a lot bigger than it looks from the outside.

The great and the good have drunk and eaten here over the years. We need hardly mention Dickens, but also Mark Twain, Sir Arthur Conan Doyle, G.K. Chesterton, P.G. Wodehouse and a host of other familiar literary characters have all been here at some point.

As is typical of Samuel Smith, their pricing is a good deal cheaper than many other places in London. You may not have a huge choice of beers (Smith's or, well, Smith's), but Old Brewery Bitter goes down well, and it's nice to get a reasonable amount of change from a £5 note.

This isn't a Grade II Listed Building for nothing, and it's one of the pubs on the Campaign For Real Ale's National Inventory of Historic Pub Interiors. After a few minutes inside it, you'll realise why.

THE ROYAL OAK

HOW TO GET THERE

The nearest underground station to The Royal Oak, and indeed several other pubs covered in this book, is Borough on the Bank branch of the Northern line.

If you're on the Charing Cross branch and heading south, change trains at Kennington and come back the two stops to Borough on the Bank branch. If you're heading north on the Charing Cross branch, you'll need to change at Euston and travel seven stops south on the Bank branch.

The Royal Oak is a fairly straightforward pub to find. Stepping out of the one exit at Borough Station you should cross over to the other side of Borough High Street, which is immediately in front of you. Turn left and take a few paces to Great Dover Street, and then turn right. At some point you'll need to cross over Great Dover Street, but no point in doing it just yet.

When you can see Silvester Street on the left, it's time to start thinking about getting over to the other side, because the next street coming up is Nebraska Street. Turning left down there will take you to the junction with Tabard Street, and The Royal Oak is on the corner where Nebraska Street meets Tabard Street.

LOCAL INFORMATION

When you reach Tabard Street, you're following in some very ancient footsteps. It used to be known as Kent Street, and is roughly lined up with an old Roman road that would take you to Canterbury via Greenwich, and then on to Dover. Its name changed from Kent Street to Tabard Street in 1877, but you wouldn't have wanted to live there at the time. It would be another ten years before various tenements were swept away, taking with them the rogues and vagabonds who used to live there.

Borough High Street, which you crossed over on the way to the pub, is also pretty much aligned with another Roman road. Until Westminster Bridge was completed in 1750, Borough High Street led to the only way to get from south of the Thames to north of it and on into the heart of London, short of taking a boat. That was, and indeed still is, London Bridge.

As a major thoroughfare, it was inevitable that many coaching inns would spring up, and at their peak there were 23 of them. We'll be visiting one of them, The George, elsewhere in this book.

44 Tabard St, London SE1 4JU
Open: Mon-Fri 11am-11pm, Sat noon-11pm, Sun noon-9pm
Tel: 020 7357 7173
https://www.harveys.org.uk/pubs/the-royal-oak-london

DESCRIPTION

Ever wondered how many pubs are called The Royal Oak? According to the website Pubs Galore, there are 465 of them, putting it in third place behind The Crown (544) and The Red Lion (585).

This Victorian pub, with its magnificent tiled frontage, is a first class example of an old-fashioned back street London boozer. No pretensions about it, no ideas above its station, it aims to be nothing more than a pub that you'd be happy to sit in and while away a few hours. The décor is lived-in scruffy, although there are some nice touches like the wooden doors with their etched glass windows that divide one bar from another.

The pub is owned by Harvey's Brewery of Lewes in Sussex, and so the majority of the drinks are their own. It's the only pub that Harvey's runs in London, which means that it's one of the few places where you can get their beers, including some difficult to get hold of bottled beers. If Sussex Best Bitter is your thing, you'll be in the right place.

SIMON THE TANNER

HOW TO GET THERE

The nearest station to Simon the Tanner is Borough on the Northern line. Moreover, it's on the part of the Northern line that splits into two sections, and you'll need the section that goes via Bank, not Charing Cross.

    The two parts of the line divide at Euston to the north and Kennington to the south, so your best plan is to aim for one or the other of those. If you find yourself on the wrong branch of the Northern line by mistake, the easiest thing to do is to change at Charing Cross and catch the Bakerloo line to Elephant and Castle. From there it's one stop north on the Northern line to Borough.

    There's only one exit at Borough. When you reach the street you should see a sign for Borough High Street on the wall opposite you. Cross over, and turn left. In front of you is the church of St. George the Martyr, so cross over Great Dover Street. Walk up to the side of the church, and turn right. This will bring you to Long Lane. Bear left when you reach Long Lane, and from here it will take you just over five minutes to reach the pub, which you'll find on the left.

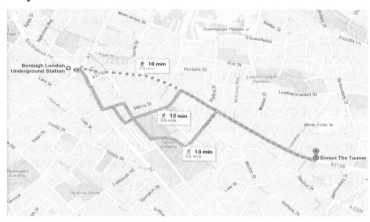

LOCAL INFORMATION

There's quite a Charles Dickens connection around here. In his book Little Dorrit, the eponymous Dorrit was baptised in the church of St. George the Martyr, and Little Dorrit's Playground is a small open space just across Borough High Street from the church.

Dickens used to live in the area, on Lant Street, while his father languished in a nearby debtor's prison. When later writing Little Dorrit in the 1850s, this had a major impact on the book. The playground opened in 1902, but suffered horribly during the Second World War. It re-emerged in something like its present form in 2001, thanks to the hard work of some local mums.

And just who was St. George the Martyr? He was, of course, THE St. George, patron saint of England, and the man responsible for many a pub name (there's one in Borough, which is covered elsewhere in this book). Much has been written about St. George and his dislike of dragons, so we'll leave that for another time and head swiftly to the pub.

231 Long Lane, London SE1 4PR
Open: Mon 5-11pm, Tue-Sat noon-11pm, Sun noon-10.30pm
Food: Mon-Sat till 10pm, Sun till 8pm
Tel: 020 7357 8740
http://simonthetanner.co.uk

DESCRIPTION

Simon the Tanner is another saint, and his name also serves as a reminder that tanning used to be a major industry in the area. A tanner, in case you don't know, is somebody who takes animal hide and processes it into leather.

The pub in its present form has only been open since 2011, as it was closed for quite some time before undergoing a major refurbishment. The result of this is a lot of wood (floors, bar, tables, chairs) and a generally functional appearance that serves its purpose as a beer-focused mid-terraced venue, although there's plenty of British food as well.

It's a Grade II Listed building, and is one of several in the area owned by United St Saviour, a local charity that helps to support Southwark pensioners. By popping in for a drink you're doing your bit for charity, and that's got to be a good thing. There's a fine selection of draught beers from all over the world including, on one of our visits, craft breweries in London, Belgium and Germany. The bottled list is equally international, and both might keep you coming back for more. Well, it worked for us.

BREWDOG CAMDEN

HOW TO GET THERE

The chances of finding the pub look quite alarming when you first step out of the tube station at Camden Town, but as long as you remember to turn left after the ticket barriers so that you're on Kentish Town Road, everything will be OK.

Camden Town is on the Northern line, and all branches of the line go through Camden, which means that you'll be fine if you're on the Northern line travelling either north or south. Mornington Crescent tube station also isn't too far away, heading south down Camden High Street, and that's about a 7-8 minute walk to BrewDog Camden.

Having turned left after the barriers, you'll see a pub called The World's End off to your right. Cross over the road towards The World's End and follow it around to your right, which will bring you on to Greenland Road. You'll need to walk along Greenland Road until you come to Bayham Street on your right, so turn into that street and follow it until you reach BrewDog Camden on the corner of Bayham Street and Greenland Street (there are several different Greenlands around here).

LOCAL INFORMATION

You walk down Bayham Street to get to BrewDog, which is where Charles Dickens used to live in the 1820s. Many other well-known people have lived around here over the years, such as Beryl Bainbridge, Alan Bennett, Dylan Thomas and Amy Winehouse. The band Madness also have plenty of local connections. There are numerous musical links to a pub called The Dublin Castle, which isn't too far away from Camden Town tube station, and although the pub's musical tradition is a strong and proud one, the beers are, well, let's be polite and say 'functional'.

If your musical knowledge begins and ends with The Animals (or the Penguin Café Orchestra, for that matter), you might prefer to spend some time visiting London Zoo, which is in Regent's Park and is only a 10-minute walk away to the west of Camden. The Zoo opened in 1828, but as it was originally intended purely for the scientific study of animals, it was almost 20 years before the general public were allowed in. Today it receives over one million visitors a year.

113 Bayham St, London NW1 0AG
Open: Mon-Thu noon-11.30pm, Fri-Sat noon-midnight,
Sun noon-10.30pm
Tel: 020 7284 4626
https://www.brewdog.com/bars/uk/camden

DESCRIPTION

There are many people who disapprove of BrewDog, specifically some of their marketing stunts and the occasional ill-thought press release, but nobody can deny that they are capable of making jolly good beer.

The brewery was founded near Aberdeen in 2007, and opened its first bar there in 2010. The first bar outside Scotland was BrewDog Camden, which opened in 2011 and was launched in their usual subtle fashion by the two founders of the brewery being driven around Camden in a tank. Today, there are numerous BrewDog bars all around the world. They tend to follow a similar format in appearance, being strictly industrial in design and looking nothing like a typical pub. Pinball tables, vintage arcade games and plenty of board games are all common throughout the pubs.

But what about the beer? Check the strength of anything before you buy it, because while you might get a gloriously refreshing Dead Pony pale ale at 3.8%, you might get lucky and find Tactical Nuclear Penguin (animals are a recurring theme) on sale at a whopping 32% ABV. It tastes really great and is by no means the strongest beer they've ever brewed.

THE PELT TRADER

HOW TO GET THERE

Part of the Bloomsbury Leisure Group Ltd, which is responsible for several other pubs in this book (Euston Tap, The Resting Hare, Waterloo Tap, Holborn Whippet), the curiously-named Pelt Trader can be found just around the corner from Cannon Street tube and mainline stations.

Travelling by tube you'll want either the District or Circle line, as they both pass through Cannon Street. It's on the southern part of the Circle line, so you can gain easy access from Westminster to make your journey in an anti-clockwise direction and from Liverpool Street to travel around in a clockwise direction.

District line travellers have plenty of options, as Cannon Street is on the section of the line from Gloucester Road to Upminster that doesn't branch off in one direction or another.

By tube, you'll need to leave via the Dowgate Hill exit. Turn left and a short stroll of a minute or less will see The Pelt Trader coming into view on the left. If you've come by train, go out of the front of the station, turn left, and then take the first left. Don't miss the pub as the entrance is small and easily passed by. And you really don't want to do that.

LOCAL INFORMATION

If you've got a few minutes to spare before heading to the pub, you've got the chance to view the site of a major piece of London history, and it will only take you two or three minutes to get there from the Dowgate Hill exit. Turn right out of the exit until you reach Cloak Lane on your left. Walk along here and turn left when you reach College Hill. Look for house number 20. The blue plaque on the wall reads: 'The house of Richard Whittington, Mayor of London, stood on this site 1423'.

Better known today by the folk tales surrounding Dick Whittington and his cat, the real Sir Richard Whittington actually came from wealthy stock, and had no need to find the streets of London paved with gold. He was sent to London from Gloucestershire to learn the trade of cloth merchant, and became immensely wealthy as a result of it. He made numerous generous gifts to the City of London, was Mayor four times, and managed to fit in being Sheriff of London and a Member of Parliament too.

Arch 3, Dowgate Hill, London EC4N 6AP
Open: Mon-Fri noon-11pm
Tel: 020 7160 0253
http://pelttrader.co.uk

DESCRIPTION

But back to the pub. A yellow neon sign above a rather plain entrance doesn't inspire much confidence in the place, and even walking inside to the largely open main bar area isn't particularly overwhelming, as it looks as if they're still building it. However, when you get to the bar and see the large array of dispensers on the back wall, things start to look up.

There are at least 16 craft cask and keg beers to choose from, and an admirable collection of bottled beers from around the world. And boy, can it get busy. You're advised to arrive mid-afternoon between the twin peaks of lunchtime and early evening, or leave it until later on at night. They've now got a license for people to consume drinks on the pavements outside, which somewhat alleviates the pressure.

No problems with service when we were last there, though, and the Dance First stout from the Pig and Porter Brewery in Tunbridge Wells was almost black with a creamy head, had a slightly smoky hint to it, with chocolate nose and taste subtly prominent. It was very smooth, and went down a treat.

CITTIE OF YORKE

HOW TO GET THERE

Chancery Lane is the closest underground station to the Cittie of Yorke, and it's on the Central line (the red one) nestling between Holborn to the west and St Paul's to the east. Tottenham Court Road and Oxford Circus are just two and three stops away respectively if you're coming from the west, and Liverpool Street is only three stops away to the east. All three of these stations are on the Central line.

You shouldn't have any problems finding the Cittie of Yorke. Leaving by exit 1 puts you on the north side of High Holborn and west of Gray's Inn Road. Walk straight ahead, leaving the wonderful half-timbered black and white building known as Staple Inn behind you for now. Another pub in this book, Ye Olde Mitre, is close by, and that entry has a few comments to make about Staple Inn.

Keep moving forward, and in less than a minute you should see Cittie of Yorke on your right. It looks grand enough from the outside, but just wait until you get inside the main bar!

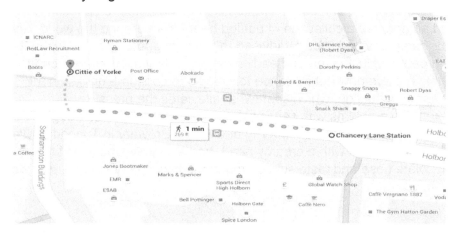

LOCAL INFORMATION

Lincoln's Inn Fields isn't too far from here. Carry on past the pub and keep going until you see a Wetherspoon's pub called Penderel's Oak on the other side of the road. Cross over (there's a handy set of traffic lights just past the pub), and almost opposite the lights you'll see a small alleyway called Great Turnstile. Go down there until it becomes Newman's Row, and after a short stroll along that road you'll see Lincoln's Inn Fields in front of you and slightly to the right.

Designed by Inigo Jones in the 17th century, this 11-acre enclosed square is a delight to stroll around. Lincoln's Inn itself is one of the four Inns of Court (Middle Temple, Inner Temple, and Gray's Inn are the others), and it's a safe bet that many of the people you see will be barristers or training to be barristers. Either that or visiting barristers in the many chambers that exist around here.

Visitors are more than welcome to stroll around the gardens, but it's best to come between 7am and 7pm from Monday to Friday. Outside those hours you'll find yourself negotiating access with gate staff.

22 High Holborn, London WC1V 6BN
Open: Mon-Sat noon-11pm
Tel: 020 7242 7670
Website: None

DESCRIPTION

Rather astonishingly, given its appearance, this pub was rebuilt in the 1920s, although buildings have stood on the site for centuries. Even the name Cittie of Yorke is new, having only been given to the pub in 1979 when it was taken over by Samuel Smith's brewery.

It used to be a coffee house prior to becoming a pub again, as it was when it was first built, and that is reflected in the wooden booths that you'll find inside. Step inside and you're in a short corridor, and before visiting any of the other rooms in the pub, carry on until you enter the main bar at the back of the pub. It's like stepping into a timbered church, complete with high vaulted ceiling. The wooden booths can be found on the right hand side of the bar, and your eye will probably be caught by the large vats that sit above and beside the long bar.

There's also a separate front bar and a cellar bar, but the latter isn't always available. It's even more unusual to see the beer garden open at the back.

Being Samuel Smith's, you are going to be drinking their own products, as they make it all themselves. Whenever we've been in the prices have been as cheap as anywhere in London. Cheers!

YE OLDE MITRE

HOW TO GET THERE

The closest underground station to Ye Olde Mitre is Chancery Lane, which is on the Central (red) line and has several exits. The easiest way to get to the pub is to use the Holborn and Gray's Inn Road East Side exit. This brings you up on High Holborn. Walk straight ahead from the tube exit, soon crossing over a junction with Brooke Street and carrying on along Holborn. You might notice some half-timbered buildings across the street. Those are collectively known as Staple Inn, and date back to the 16th century.

Remain on Holborn until Hatton Garden appears on the left. Turn into Hatton Garden, crossing the road as you do so, which will leave you standing beside a bank. Keep your wits about you here and make sure that your eyes are looking at the signs above the window displays in the various jewellery stores that you walk past. This is not out of frugality. After walking by four jewellery stores, at the same height as the shop signs you'll see a discreet sign above an alley, and it says 'Ye Olde Mitre, established 1546'. Turn into the alley and a short distance along is the pub.

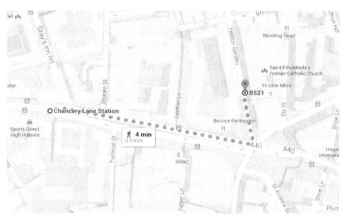

LOCAL INFORMATION

Staple Inn goes back to 1585, and was a fairly typical building for the area at that time. It's difficult to imagine Holborn full of such buildings now, although they wouldn't have had the shops at the front. They're currently leased to the present occupants, because in the past Staple Inn consisted of two separate buildings.

You don't need to look too closely to see this, but you might miss it with a quick glance. Look at the top of the right-hand side of the building, and you'll see that the two right-most bays are different from the five on the left. This is because the two at the right belonged to a private house-hold built in very much the same style as Staple Inn.

If you go through the gateway at the front of it, you'll find yourself in a courtyard with the Staple Inn Hall in front of you. The Hall had to be rebuilt in the 1950s following damage sustained during the Second World War, and doesn't match up to the grandeur of the exterior. Even so, it is still a fine building in its own right.

1 Ely Place, London EC1N 6SJ
Open: Mon-Fri 11am-11pm, Sat noon-11pm, Sun noon-4pm
Tel: 020 7405 4751
www.yeoldemitreholborn.co.uk

DESCRIPTION

The entrance to the pub is through a fine wooden door, with several barrels usually scattered about the small courtyard outside. Once inside, you'll find that the main bar is relatively small, with a comfortable, lived-in feeling, plenty of wood, and lots of brewery-related objects dotted around the walls.

There is a larger seating area in another room (there are lots of rooms here), with its own separate bar and a snug room off to one side. Again, various pub-related artefacts adorn the walls, with a large collection of empty beer bottles perched high up on a number of separate shelves.

Something called The Bishop's Room can be found up a few stairs if it's all getting too crowded at ground level, and that, along with the name of the pub, gives us a clue to its origins. The original building dates back to 1546 and, according to Fuller's brewery, it's where the servants of the Bishop of Ely were housed. The current building is a relative youngster, only going back as far as the end of the 18th century.

Overall, we found it to be a charming old place, full of objects to look at and admire, and of course a fine range of Fuller's beers.

THE HARP

HOW TO GET THERE

The multi-award winning Harp has Charing Cross as its nearest underground station, and this one is served by both the Northern line (the black one) and the Bakerloo line (the brown one). Rather obviously, it is on the Charing Cross branch of the Northern line.

As long as you arrive before 9.45 in the evening you'll be able to leave the underground station by Exit 9, which places you on the north side of the Strand. Otherwise, leave by any way you can and take great care crossing the busy Strand to get to the outside of exit 9.

If you're leaving from the tube station by exit 9, turn right and follow the Strand until it splits in two at a Y-junction. Here you should take the right hand fork on to Duncannon Street. It will only take you a few seconds to get here, and immediately after the fork you'll see Adelaide Street on the right. Carry on along Adelaide Street until you reach the junction with William IV Street, and the Harp will be on the other side of the junction and almost immediately in front of you.

LOCAL INFORMATION

London is awash with landmarks, and you're not far away from one of the most famous ones of all if you're heading for The Harp, so you may as well pay it a visit. At the point where the Strand made its fork and you followed Duncannon Street on the right, remaining on Duncannon Street will take you directly to Trafalgar Square and its iconic statues.

The National Gallery forms a spectacular backdrop to the northern end of Leicester Square, and there's no excuse for not calling in because this marvellous collection is open to the public totally free of charge.

In Trafalgar Square itself, Admiral Horatio Nelson stands proud on his plinth at almost three times the size he was in real life. It celebrates his famous victory at the Battle of Trafalgar in 1805, from which the Square takes its name.

The statues of the lions are almost as famous as Nelson's Column. They were created by Sir Edward Landseer and cast by Baron Marochetti, and they turned up in 1867. The previously empty plinth in the north-west corner of the square has been the home of some weird and wonderful art installations in recent times, so check it out.

47 Chandos Place, London WC2N 4HS
Open: Mon-Thu 10.30am-11.30pm, Fri-Sat 10.30am-midnight,
Sun noon-10.30pm
Tel: 020 7836 0291
www.harpcoventgarden.com

DESCRIPTION

Fuller's took over this pub in 2014 and did very little to it. This was a very good thing (apart from losing the sausages that used to be sold here), because The Harp doesn't need changing at all. It's only small, with a separate room upstairs and overspill areas to the front and back, but it still gets packed. You'll quite often see the fine colourful etched windows at the front of the pub opened up if the weather's up to it.

There are a few bar stools dotted about downstairs, which is the only seating that you'll find there. Other than that, it's standing room only and a queue at the bar if you arrive at the wrong time. However, service has always been quick and efficient when we've been in, and a small wait lets you peruse the extensive range of beers on offer.

There are hundreds of pump clips adorning the walls, which kept us entertained, but other than that the décor is basic (think lots of wood), but that doesn't matter, because what this pub is all about is beer. Not for nothing was The Harp once voted National Pub of the Year by the Campaign For Real Ale.

THE OLD PACK HORSE

HOW TO GET THERE

The Old Pack Horse is in Chiswick, and the closest tube station to the pub is Chiswick Park, which is on the District line (the green one). If you're buying a TravelCard ticket for a day or longer, remember that Chiswick Park is in tube zone 3. That's the highest zone number that this book goes to, it never reaches the giddy heights of zone 4 or more.

The District line is the only one serving Chiswick Park, and make sure you get a tube that's going to Ealing Broadway, otherwise you'll be heading off in the wrong direction. If nothing's advertised as going there, your best bet is to go to Earl's Court and change there.

You'll need to leave the station by the left-most exit and walk a few yards to your left to a zebra crossing. Cross over, turn right, and then turn left when you reach a mini-roundabout. This will take you along Acton Lane and across a bridge over a railway line. You'll soon come to another mini-roundabout, which you'll need to go straight across and keep on walking down Acton Lane. The pub soon comes into view on the left, at the corner of Acton Lane and Chiswick High Road.

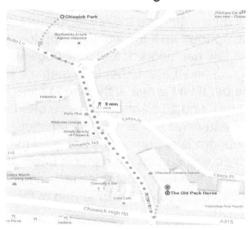

LOCAL INFORMATION

Chiswick used to be a thriving country retreat before it got swallowed up by the rest of London, and that's just what it would have been when the artist William Hogarth used to live here away from his other home in central London. He was born in 1697 and lived to the then pretty good age of 66. His old retreat is a fifteen-minute stroll from the pub, and repays a visit. To get there, carry on walking along Chiswick High Road until you see Dukes Avenue on your right. Walk along it until you reach Ellesmere Road, and then turn left. The house will appear shortly on your right.

There's a Mulberry tree in the front garden of this Grade I listed building, and astonishingly it would have been there when Hogarth was in residence. Today the house acts as a museum. Among his many famous works are Beer Street and Gin Lane, showing how beer is good for you and gin is not. And if all this culture doesn't tempt you, Fuller's Brewery is a five-minute walk away. Anyway, off to the pub.

434 Chiswick High Road, London W4 5TF
Open: Mon-Wed 11am-midnight, Thu 11am-1am,
Fri-Sat 11am-2am, Sun noon-midnight
Tel: 020 8994 2872
www.oldpackhorsechiswick.co.uk

DESCRIPTION

The Old Pack Horse looks like you'd expect a London pub to look. It's a large red-brick imposing building with some impressive tile-work, especially by the main entrance. Inside there's plenty of wood, little alcoves to retreat into, etched mirrors and windows, and a fine panelled bar with a beautiful display at the back of the bar. The pub was originally built in 1747, and you can well believe that when you step inside.

What they wouldn't have had in 1747 is a Thai food menu, but they do here. They wouldn't even have had Fuller's beers to drink, which is their loss and our gain. There are a number of guest kegs in addition to the Fuller's handpumps, and we spotted the ever-reliable Sierra Nevada Pale Ale tucked in amongst them. There's also quite a range of bottled beers.

When we arrived one Bank Holiday Monday, just as the pub was opening up and getting ready for the day, the staff described themselves as 'sleep-deprived but happy'. Well, it was a Bank Holiday, after all. They set about their work cheerfully enough, and we soon had two pints of London Pride nestling in our hands. A good, solid, London pub.

CRAFT BEER COMMON CLAPHAM

Photo courtesy of the Craft Beer Company

HOW TO GET THERE

You're going to be using the Northern line for this one, so you'll need to be travelling south towards Morden if you're arriving here from the centre of the city. If you're travelling in the opposite direction, all services stop at the pub's nearest tube station, Clapham Common.

From Clapham Common station and after leaving the platform behind, you'll need to climb up a few steps and use the south side exit to take you to The Pavement (confusingly, it's a road), then turn right and walk towards the traffic lights controlling the crossing to get to the other side of the road. You should see a large clock face at the top of a brick tower in front of you and just off to one side.

The Pavement will soon join up with Clapham High Street, and you stroll along here past Stonhouse (yes, that's how it's spelt) Street and Prescott Place until you reach Clapham Manor Street. Turn left into it and try to ignore the lure of Clapham Leisure Centre as you'll soon reach the pub on your left hand side.

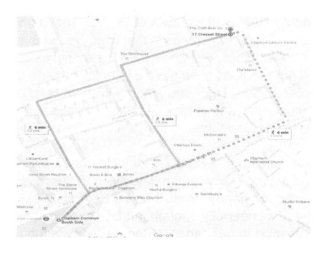

LOCAL INFORMATION

On your way to the road crossing when you first leave the station, stop and turn around to look back at the station that you've just left behind. The entrance is a Grade II listed small circular domed building dating back to 1923-4. You can thank Charles Holden for the design of this marvellous structure, and it is a credit to London Underground that it survives to this day.

However, its future may be in doubt. Clapham Common is one of only two underground stations that are not only deep underground but also have an island platform. Clapham North is the other one, and there are plans to redesign both of them owing to concerns over passenger safety. We can't argue with that, but we hope they leave the exit alone.

If you've got some time to spare, don't start walking to the pub just yet, but head off in the opposite direction from the road crossing when you leave the station exit, and you'll very soon see the Clapham Common in front of you. The Common has existed here for over 1000 years, merits a mention in the Domesday Book, and is home to the oldest and largest bandstand in London. Like the station dome, the Victorian bandstand is also a Grade II listed building.

128 Clapham Manor St, London SW4 6ED
Open: Mon-Thu 4pm-11pm, Fri 4pm-midnight, Sat noon-midnight, Sun noon-11pm
Food: Tue-Fri 5pm-10pm, Sat-Sun noon-10pm
Tel: 020 7498 9633
www.thecraftbeerco.com/clapham

DESCRIPTION

The bars really are a thing of wonder in these Craft Beer Company pubs, and Clapham doesn't let them down. An enticing array of hand pumps will greet you at the bar, normally 10 of them, and along with 20 keg lines and over 200 bottles and cans, you'll find yourself spoilt for choice.

The décor is fairly basic, with plenty of wooden floors and a few stools set around the walls, along with a small table or two, and there is some space boasting a carpet to the rear of the single bar. Get there early enough and you might be able to sink into a comfy settee.

If the weather's being kind, the astro-turfed garden area is well worth a visit, complete with its white picket fence. There's plenty of room out in the garden, which is covered, but like any good pub in London it can get very busy at times.

This feels very much like a locals' pub rather than some of the more tourist-led pubs in central London. Many online reviews report it as being welcoming and friendly, and after several visits ourselves, we can't disagree with that.

THE CROSS KEYS

HOW TO GET THERE

The nearest tube station to The Cross Keys is Covent Garden, just a three-minute stroll away. If you've emerged from the Underground on Long Acre and you can see Marks and Spencer's in front of you, all well and good. If you've somehow managed to get out on to James Street, turn left and walk the few yards to Long Acre.

Incidentally, if you're ever in Leeds and sitting in a pub called The Crowd of Favours (Leeds Brewery), if you look out of the front window of the pub you'll see a blue plaque on the wall opposite. This will tell you that Mr Marks and Mr Spencer first went into business together towards the end of the 19th century in Kirkgate Market in Leeds. There's a replica of their original Penny Bazaar in the market today, which is well worth a visit. But that's a whole other book.

Back to London. When on Long Acre head to the right past Neal Street until you see Endell Street on your left. Turning left into Endell Street, it will only be a minute or so before you're crossing Shelton Street and then The Cross Keys appears on your left.

LOCAL INFORMATION

Covent Garden is in the West End of London, and has numerous attractions close by. If transport is your thing, the London Transport Museum is just around the corner. Into opera? The Royal Opera House, home of the Royal Ballet, is also in the area, and it's only a short step away from the English National Opera. Like the theatre? You're surrounded by them: Novello, Lyceum, Adelphi, Palace, Cambridge, New London, and many, many more.

Prefer a pint? Read on.

31 Endell St, London WC2H 9BA
Open: Mon-Sat 11am-11pm, Sun noon-10.30pm
Food: Mon-Sat noon-2.30pm, Sun noon-3pm
Tel: 020 7836 5185
www.crosskeyscoventgarden.com

DESCRIPTION

Brodie's Brewery run the Cross Keys, and their spiritual home is the King William IV pub at 816 High Road in Leyton. It's another fine pub but more than a 10-minute walk from the nearest tube (Walthamstow Central) so we couldn't include it in this book. We were in there one day enjoying a marmite stout (tastes better than it sounds, trust us), when one of the brewers came into the pub to make herself a drink. While she was waiting for a kettle to boil, we exchanged a few polite comments, and then we asked her what prompted her to brew a marmite stout in the first place. Her reply was along the lines of, 'I was having breakfast one morning and I thought, why not?' Good for you.

The Cross Keys looks completely out of place from the outside, as if it's just wandered up from somewhere in the heart of rural Kent. Bedecked by flowers, with marble columns and two cherubs sitting atop the name of the pub, inside it gets even better. Just about every square inch of space is given over to Victorian clutter, mirrors, ornaments, road signs, Beatles paraphernalia, and almost anything else that you can think of. Napkin autographed by Elvis Presley? Tick.

The beer comes from Brodie's Brewery, of course. We tried a Kiwi pale ale on our most recent visit, and were delighted by it. It was light, refreshing, and at 3.8% it's very easy going. There are many pubs to see in London, but you could very easily drop anchor here.

THE NAGS HEAD

Photo courtesy of The Nags Head

HOW TO GET THERE

The nearest tube station to The Nags Head is Covent Garden. If you leave via the Long Acre exit with Marks and Spencer in front of you, turn sharp right and head down James Street. You'll soon see the pub on your left.

Covent Garden underground station is only served by the Piccadilly line and is a Grade II listed building. It opened in 1907, and if you're feeling energetic when you get off the tube you can get to street level by walking up the 193 steps that take you there. The rest of us catch the lift.

There's easy access on the Piccadilly line from the likes of King's Cross, Leicester Square, Piccadilly Circus and Earl's Court, but if you're not near a Piccadilly line station then somewhere like Leicester Square is a good place to change lines. It's served by the Northern line as well as the Piccadilly line, which calls for a bit of tube trivia. The journey between Covent Garden and Leicester Square stations is the shortest journey on the tube network at under 300 yards (274 metres) and a journey time of 45 seconds. Time it, next time.

LOCAL INFORMATION

It's hard to believe now, but back in the 16th century this area was all open fields. Henry VIII, who helped himself to anything that was going, took hold of the land and granted it to the Earl of Bedford in 1552. Gradually bars, markets, theatres and brothels began to spring up, probably not quite what Henry had in mind, but it all sorted itself out in the end and is now the district that you find yourself in today.

There's still a wealth of entertainment to be had here. It's very much the theatre centre of London, with more venues than you can shake a stick at, if (as Groucho Marx said) that's your idea of a good time. If opera's your thing, then the Royal Opera House and the English National Opera are a short stride away. The Thames rolls serenely along to the South, and if you make a diversion along the way to The Harp public house (described elsewhere in this book), then who could blame you?

> 10 James St, London WC2E 8BT
> Open: Sun-Thu 9am-11pm, Fri-Sat 9am-midnight
> Food: Sun-Thu 9am-10pm, Fri-Sat 9am-5pm
> Tel: 020 7836 4678
> www.mcmullens.co.uk/nagshead

DESCRIPTION

The Nags Head is one of only four pubs in the centre of London run by McMullen's Brewery, who are based in Hertfordshire. They've been going since 1827, so you can be assured that they're getting the hang of it by now. What they're not getting the hang of is this pub's name. You'll see it in the pub itself and on their website as both The Nag's Head and The Nags Head. We've omitted the apostrophe, even though there's a glut of them on the market.

Inside you'll find a nice, spacious boozer, and it can get very busy at times, but there always seems to be somewhere to sit down. It's not pretentious, and it does its job well. The beers are satisfying without ever really being ground-breaking, but there are times when you need a drink like that. Although, if you see their lightly-hopped AK XXX on sale when you visit then do try some. It's a fine bitter that's brewed to a recipe that's older than your grandparents. And escaping from the chaos of Covent Garden and sitting down with a pint of Bard Of Ale and letting it all pass you by, is one of the huge pleasures in life.

THE BLACKBIRD

HOW TO GET THERE

Earl's Court is the nearest tube station to The Blackbird. It's on the District (green) and Piccadilly (dark blue) lines, and makes for easy access from many parts of London. Unlike some stations, all Piccadilly line services stop here, so you don't have to worry about missing the stop.

You'll need to head for the exit that's marked Earl's Court Road, and when you arrive at street level it really couldn't get any easier. Turn right, walk down Earl's Court Road, and within one minute The Blackbird will appear on your left hand side on the opposite side of the road. Take any opportunity that you can to cross over the road, as it always seems to be very busy.

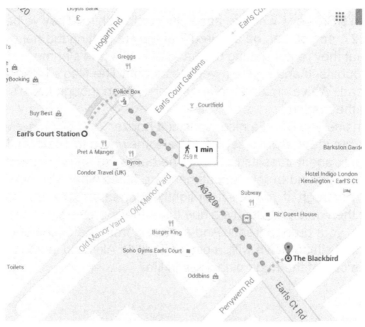

LOCAL INFORMATION

If you haven't crossed over the road by now, you'll see a little passageway called Old Manor Yard on your right, a few doorways along from the tube station. This gives us a clue as to how the station, and the surrounding area, got its name. The manor part of the name is from a manor court, which was the lowest court of law going back over a thousand years, and it was ruled by the lord of the manor. Judgements arising from the court only applied to those people who lived within the manor or held territory there.

The Earls of Oxford were the top dogs in town back in the day, when what is now Earl's Court was all green fields and pastures, and they even get a mention in the Domesday Book in 1086. It was the Earls who took charge of the manor court, and hence Earl's Court.

Many famous people have lived here over the years, and blue plaques abound on the walls of nearby buildings. The composer Benjamin Britten has one, as does Alfred Hitchcock and the comedy actress Hattie Jacques. Perhaps the most famous former resident was Diana, Princess of Wales, who lived for a brief period at nearby 60 Colehorne Court on Old Brompton Road prior to her engagement to Prince Charles.

209 Earls Court Rd, London SW5 9AN
Open: Mon-Wed 9am-11pm, Thu-Sat 9am-11.30pm, Sun 9am-10.30pm
Tel: 020 7835 1855
www.blackbirdearlscourt.co.uk

DESCRIPTION

The doorway to the pub is flanked by two fine marble columns and leads you into a light and airy room which will instantly make lovers of chandeliers feel at home. The large, plain windows give the place a sense of light, and the whole room is nicely functional. There are little alcoves to go and sit in, barstools around the walls with a shelf to rest your pint, wooden tables and chairs dotted about, and a fine carpeted dining area at the back of the pub. This is a Fuller's pub, so you'll know what to expect. There were no guest ales on when we were there, but we happily settled on a splendid pint of ESB.

They serve a wide range of food here, and the pub speciality is pies. Lots of them, including a rather fine steak pie made using Fuller's London Pride. And speaking of pies, there was a rather splendid notice on a blackboard attached to a wall near where we sat on our last visit. It read: 'Well behaved children welcome. The rest will be made into pies'.

THE SHIP AND SHOVELL

Photo courtesy of The Ship and Shovell

HOW TO GET THERE

Although The Ship and Shovell is listed in this book alongside Embankment tube station, Charing Cross is almost the same distance away, so choose whichever is the more convenient.

Embankment is on the Circle (yellow) and District (green) lines. Leave by the Villiers Street exit and walk straight ahead. Walk up Villiers Street towards Charing Cross until you see a pub called the Princess of Wales on your right. No, it's not named after the late Diana, this is in honour of the wife of King George IV. The story of their lives is the stuff of novels, soap operas, and reality shows, and is rich in detail. Illegal marriages, separations, lovers, illegitimate children, it's all going on.

Anyway, having found the Princess of Wales pub (a good Nicholson's pub), you'll see signs for The Arches Shopping on your left. This leads you into an alleyway past restaurants, shops and nightclubs. If you're coming from Charing Cross, on either the Northern (black) or Bakerloo (brown) lines, find exit 2 for Villiers Street, turn right and walk down the street until you find The Arches Shopping on your right, and then turn right and stroll along the alleyway until you reach the steps leading up to the pub.

LOCAL INFORMATION

When you get to the top of the steps you'll find a pub on your right and a pub on your left - and it's the same pub. Until The Euston Tap acquired The Cider Tap, The Ship and Shovell was the only pub we knew that exists on two sides of the same street, two separate buildings that each have their own bar.

Both buildings are managed by Badger Brewery, owned by Hall and Woodhouse. The company can date itself back to 1777, when Charles Hall set up a brewery in Ansty in Dorset. His son Robert made his nephew Edward Woodhouse a partner some 60 years later, and the company continues as Hall and Woodhouse to this day.

Hall and Woodhouse, if you're reading this, can we issue a request? Make Poacher's Choice a cask or keg beer, instead of only being available in bottles. It's a superb liquorice and damson flavoured beer, quite strong at 5.7% ABV, and we've yet to introduce it to someone who doesn't like it.

Oh, and the double 'LL' in the pub name? The pub is named after Sir Cloudesley Shovell, who had a distinguished naval career in the 17th century until it all went a bit wrong. Everything he sailed on sank, but he's still got his portrait on the sign hanging outside the pub.

1-3 Craven Passage, London WC2N 5PH
Open: Mon-Sat 11am-11pm, Sun closed
Food: Mon-Fri noon-3.30pm, Sat noon-4pm
Tel: 020 7839 1311
http://shipandshovell.co.uk

DESCRIPTION

Hall and Woodhouse has been in the hands of the same family for generations, and the multi-great-grandchildren of the people who founded it are still running the company today. This shows through in their pubs.

The smaller of the two bars is full of wooden alcoves, and makes for a welcome retreat from the main bar on the other side of the road, which can get very busy indeed. Having said that, you can usually find a table to take care of you and your drink if you walk far enough towards the back of the pub. Not surprisingly, the majority of beers on sale in this lovely Victorian boozer come from the Badger Brewery. If you're lucky, you'll get to try a beer called Tanglefoot.

There's a nice tale behind the name of that particular beer. The head brewer, John Woodhouse, was inviting his team to sample the latest brew, and as he got up to leave the room he found his legs tangled up in the lead of his pet dog. One stumble later, and the then new beer had got its name.

THE EUSTON TAP

HOW TO GET THERE

Amazingly enough, The Euston Tap is very close to Euston Station. All manner of transport is linked to Euston, including mainline railways and the London Overground, but for our purposes the two underground lines that pass through here are the Northern and the Victoria.

Euston is on both branches of the northern part of the Northern line, so no need to worry about being on the correct one. The Victoria line is also convenient for various parts of London, like Victoria and Oxford Circus.

To get from the station to The Euston Tap without running the risk of getting struck down by a bus, we usually take the long way around. Leave the tube station and at the top of the escalators turn right to exit from the mainline station. In front of you will be an array of shops, bars and restaurants, but ignore all that for now and turn sharp right to walk by the front of the station. This will take you to Melton Street, where you need to turn left and stroll towards the large junction that brings up Euston Road. Turn left before crossing over the road, and from there it's just a short walk to the Tap.

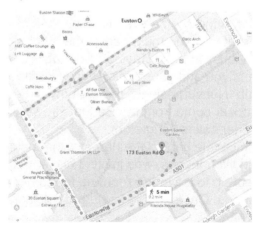

LOCAL INFORMATION

Euston Tap looks peculiar when you first see it, as it is formed inside one of two Lodge Buildings that are just about all that remain visible of the old Euston Station that was demolished in the early 1960s. Lists of destinations served by the earlier station are embedded in panels around the arch. The lodge opposite used to be The Cider Tap but since November 2016 has become a second bar for the Euston Tap - and serving some different beers, note.

There has been a station on this site since 1837, although for seven years an Act of Parliament meant that trains had to be pulled out of the station and couldn't run under their own steam. As more and more trains started to use it, the station expanded piecemeal, but there was no major overhaul of it until the 1960s.

Many millions of people use this station, and the Underground can be thanked for almost 15 million people entering and exiting the station in any one year. Fortunately they don't all drink in Euston Tap, as it is rather small.

190 Euston Road, London NW1 2EF
Open: Mon-Fri 3pm-11pm, Sat noon-11pm, Sun 2pm-9pm
Tel: 020 3137 8837
www.eustontap.com

DESCRIPTION

One thing must be made clear before entering the bar: you are not here for creature comforts. This is easily verified by clambering up the rickety spiral staircase to the upstairs seating area and the toilets, although the latter are improving over time.

What you are here for is beer, and this place has lots of it. There are usually 8 cask ales and 20 more on keg, served from dispensers mounted into the wall at the back of the bar.

The pub is bigger than it looks from the outside, but it can still get uncomfortably busy at times. There is some overspill outside into an open area and beer garden, with a number of tables dotted about the place, so you should manage to find somewhere to perch your drink.

When you first walk in you'll see the bar in front of you, with two very short walkways either side of it leading to two fridges containing a fine selection of global bottled beers. Above the fridges are two blackboards telling you what's on offer from the dispensers behind the bar, and they make for interesting reading and probably quite a bit of decision-making as to which drink you're going to buy. Or buy first, should we say.

THE EXMOUTH ARMS

HOW TO GET THERE

The best tube station for The Exmouth Arms is Euston, on the Victoria (light blue) and Northern (black) lines. This gives you direct access to and from the likes of Camden Town, King's Cross, Waterloo, Charing Cross, Oxford Circus, Victoria and many others.

On leaving the underground at the top of the escalators and stepping on to the mainline station concourse, turn right to head outside and then turn immediately right again, ignoring the temptations of the shops and restaurants in front of you. Passing alongside the front of the station, go down the steps to reach Melton Street, and cross over using the handy zebra crossing.

Euston Street is almost immediately opposite the steps that you've just come down, and you need to walk along it until you reach The Bree Louise on your right. You could pause for refreshment here of course, but to get to The Exmouth Arms you'll need to turn right into Cobourg Street (The Bree Louise is still on your right) and keep going past the pub until you reach Starcross Street on the left. The Exmouth Arms is located at 1 Starcross Street, so you can't really miss it.

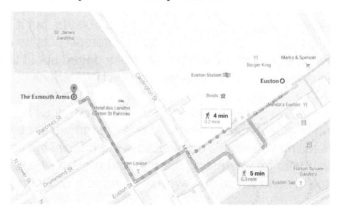

LOCAL INFORMATION

Even though Euston Square looks rather new in places, it was first opened back in 1863, when it was known as Gower Street station. Gower Street lies nearby, and makes for a less confusing name in our view, but it was changed to Euston Square in 1909. These origins mean that Euston Square tube station is actually older than Euston tube station, which always surprises us.

You're very close to The Euston Tap here, which is another pub featured in this book, and the walk to the Exmouth Arms will take you alongside a pub that didn't quite make it this time around. That's not to stop you going in, of course, and many people rate The Bree Louise very highly, but we feel it has been letting itself down a little bit lately, compared to former glories. Hopefully, things will improve.

1 Starcross St, London NW1 2HR
Open: Sun-Thu 9am-11pm, Fri-Sat 9am-midnight
Tel: 020 7387 5440
www.publove.co.uk/exmouth-arms-euston

DESCRIPTION

The first thing to do on getting here is to ignore the doorway with the rather garish 'pub' sign in the window, and walk around the corner to the main entrance. Once inside, you'll see a row of tables and benches in front of you, and to the right are two lines of tables and chairs, with the line nearest the bar being traditional wooden chairs and the one nearest the window being fitted with back-to-back padded benches.

The walls contain a lot of exposed brickwork, which works like a charm on people like us, who are always pleased to see such a thing, and the floor is a pleasant mix of tiles and wood. The wooden panelled bar is the next thing to catch your eye, and it has a pretty good range of cask and keg ales. You'll also find an impressive collection of bottled beers behind the bar, under the simple heading 'beer'.

It's not the most decorative or ornate pub that we've ever been in, but that can sometimes work to your advantage. This is definitely a craft pub, and it even has its own 'burger craft' food section.

THE RESTING HARE

HOW TO GET THERE

The Resting Hare is one of a number of pubs in this book that stand close to Euston underground station, which is on both branches of the Northern (black) line. It's also on the Victoria (light blue) line.

After making your way through the maze of tunnels that lead you from the underground platform to the escalators heading for the mainline station, turn right to exit the station from the top of the escalators, and then immediately left when you reach fresh air.

Using Marks & Spencer as a guide, walk past the store and down some steps onto Eversholt Street. Turn right here until you reach the Euston Road. Cross by the traffic lights and you're on Upper Woburn Place. Here you'll have to employ traffic lights again, because you want to be on the same side of Upper Woburn Place as St Pancras Parish Church, which is the large church that you can see in front of you.

Having safely crossed over, turn right and walk along Upper Woburn Place with the church on your left, and you'll soon come to a passageway called Woburn Walk. Go down it a short way and you'll see The Resting Hare on your right.

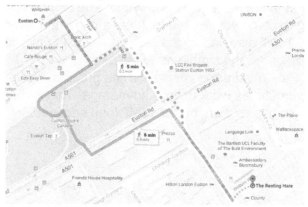

LOCAL INFORMATION

The Resting Hare is an unusual name. Fortunately, a plaque on the wall of the pub tells the charming story behind the inspiration for the name. And we quote:

The architect behind Woburn Walk, Thomas Cubitt, noted the tameness of the hares on his early morning constitutional. After the opening of Woburn Walk, the newly laid paving stones became a magnet for the local hares, who could easily be seen late at night resting peacefully along the walk.

Indeed, famous poet W. B. Yeats who lived on Woburn Walk in the 1920's, wrote of 'a handsome old grey hare taking rest' outside number 6.

Development and increased traffic on the Euston road had made the crossing too difficult for the hares, and by the start of the 1930's they had disappeared into history.

So now you know!

Woburn Walk 8- London, 11 Upper Woburn Place, London WC1H 0JW
Open: Mon-Sat noon-11pm, Sun closed
Tel: 020 3137 6434
www.restinghare.com

DESCRIPTION

The Resting Hare is part of the same company that includes The Euston Tap, The Holborn Whippet, The Waterloo Tap and The Pelt Trader. There are others outside London as well, and they all have one thing in common: plenty of beer choice.

The buildings vary quite a lot in design, and this one is pretty spacious (unlike The Euston Tap!) with an outside seating area, although we felt it could do with a few more tables inside, as there is a fair amount of standing space. That said, it was comfortable enough every time we've been in, although it can get busy in the early evenings as beer-savvy commuters enjoy a pint or two before making the journey home from Euston Station.

There were ten keg lines and four cask ales on when we last paid it a visit, and it was good to be served a pint in a custom glass with 'The Resting Hare' etched on it below a sketch of a hare. The walls also contained various images of hares, lending a nice touch to the overall décor and a refreshing change from the usual collection of pub memorabilia.

CRAFT BEER COMPANY CLERKENWELL

HOW TO GET THERE

Google is being more than a little difficult when it comes to finding your way to this pub from Farringdon, which is the nearest tube station to The Craft Beer Company. It insists on a particular route, and won't let us change it to be the path that we suggest you use. Every time we try altering it, Google insists on putting in a ridiculous detour that takes you all over the place. Because Greville Street is one-way, it seems Google won't allow you to walk along the pavement in the wrong direction!

You can get to Farringdon on the Metropolitan, Circle, and Hammersmith and City lines. When you leave the station, you'll see a pub called The Castle on your left. Don't go in but instead turn right and walk along Cowcross Street until you reach the junction with Farringdon Road.

This is where we and Google disagree. Our preferred route is to cross over Farringdon Road and walk along Greville Street. When you reach Hatton Garden turn right and keep walking until you reach a junction with Hatton Wall, at which point turn left. The pub will soon appear on the left.

LOCAL INFORMATION

Hatton Garden has been the centre of London's jewellery trade for centuries. The street is named after Sir Christopher Hatton, who was gifted a house in the area by Queen Elizabeth I towards the end of the 16th century. The two were rumoured to be lovers, although there's no proof of this. Nonetheless, she bestowed numerous gifts on Sir Christopher, often to the outrage of others. In this case, it was the Bishop of Ely who was outraged. After all, it had been his house. It was situated on Ely Place, the last street in London to be in private hands.

Ely Place itself is worth a look. On the way to the pub, when you get to Hatton Garden turn left instead of right, take another left when you get to Charterhouse Street, and yet another left into Ely Place. Ye Olde Mitre pub, also in this book, is at 1 Ely Place. Further along from that pub you'll find St Etheldreda's Roman Catholic Church, named after the saint who founded the Ely monastery in 673. The church is one of the oldest buildings in London, built sometime around the middle of the 13th century.

82 Leather Ln, London EC1N 7TR
Open: Mon-Sat noon-11pm, Sun noon-10.30pm
Tel: 020 7404 7049
http://thecraftbeerco.com

DESCRIPTION

From one of London's oldest buildings, we arrive at one of its newest pubs. The Craft Beer Company first opened in this part of London in July 2011. Décor is sparse but comfortable, with a wooden floor and a few tables dotted about the place. Bar snacks are available, but this pub's main function is very clear as soon as you step inside. It's all about the beer.

The long bar has an arresting display of pump clips, 16 cask beers last time we went in, and a similar number of keg ones, with various interesting bottles behind the bar. You'll be spoilt for choice here, that's for sure. Our one grumble is that you might have to peer at every pump clip before ordering a drink, as we've never seen a handy blackboard or monitor displaying the names, prices, strengths etc. of every beer. The Grove in Huddersfield, or The Wellington in Birmingham, are two places that spring to mind, both of which handle information about their beers particularly well. However, you might just plunge in and buy the first thing that you look at. Works for us!

THE CROWN TAVERN

HOW TO GET THERE

Farringdon is on the Circle, Metropolitan, and Hammersmith and City lines, so a little trundle around the Circle line will get you there from most parts of London. Easy access is also gained by travelling to King's Cross and changing there. Don't be fooled by the proximity of Farringdon to King's Cross Station on the Underground map, as you're better off catching any of the three lines that serve Farringdon unless you fancy a half hour's brisk walk.

On leaving the tube station you should turn left down Cowcross Street. You'll soon see a pub called The Castle, but ignore that one as it looks better than it acts, and instead turn left in front of The Castle and head up Turnmill Street.

You keep on Turnmill Street by some interestingly named side streets like Turk's Head Yard and Dicken's Mews (he gets everywhere) until you come to a junction with Clerkenwell Road. You need to go directly across here and continue up what is now Farringdon Lane on the other side. First right is Vine Street Bridge, so head down there until you reach Clerkenwell Street. At this point The Crown Tavern will be looming large in front of you.

LOCAL INFORMATION

There are a number of other pubs in the vicinity of The Crown Tavern, so depending on how far you want to walk you might also take in The Jerusalem Tavern, Ye Olde Mitre, The Craft Beer Company (the one on 82 Leather Lane), and so on. However, we don't want to lead you astray - well, not too astray - so perhaps we should focus on such things as Saint Etheldreda's Church (which is actually very close to Ye Olde Mitre!)

Closer to hand along Clerkenwell Close, you'll find St. James's Church Garden, which is worth a bit of an explore. St James's Church can be found here, not surprisingly, and beneath it lies the Crypt on The Green, which is available for hire along with The Well and The Vestry. Must make for some interesting corporate meetings.

43 Clerkenwell Green, London EC1R 0EG
Open: Mon-Fri 10am-11.30pm, Sat-Sun noon-11.30pm
Tel: 020 7253 4973
www.thecrowntavernec1.co.uk

DESCRIPTION

The pub is a former concert hall going back to the 18th century when the Apollo Concert Room was on the first floor, and is suitably decorative inside including some marvellous ornate mirrors. On a previous visit it had been surrounded by scaffolding, but that had all gone on a subsequent trip and a spruced-up pub had emerged.

There's a garden outside (well, garden might be stretching it a bit, let's call it tables and chairs), which had more people in it than the pub on a sunny Friday afternoon. There probably weren't too many of them looking at the Marx Memorial Library, but it's just across from the garden.

Back inside, and it's always nice to see Dark Star's Hop Head on tap, and you can usually expect to see five different ales to choose from, alongside a host of keg and bottled offerings. With a number of separate drinking areas to wander around, you can choose your spot and admire the décor while supping your drink of choice.

And do check their website for details of events. We missed their contribution to the UK Keg Craft Beer Showcase by days. Grr!

THE JERUSALEM TAVERN

HOW TO GET THERE

Farringdon is the nearest tube station for The Jerusalem Tavern, which places us on the Hammersmith and City line (pink), the Circle line (yellow) and the Metropolitan line (magenta). King's Cross is only one station away, Euston Square is two stops, and Baker Street, Marylebone and Paddington are not too far away to the west. Liverpool Street is three stops away to the east, and if you're anywhere near a Circle line station then you can just jump on a tube and trundle around the line until it gets to Farringdon.

During peak travel time there is an exit from Farringdon underground station that takes you out on to Turnmill Street, but if you're travelling at any other time then you'll take the main exit to Cowcross Street. Turn left on leaving the station and walk towards the Castle pub. No need to go in it, simply use it as a marker and turn left onto Turnmill Street.

After walking a short way down Turnmill Street, turn right into Benjamin Street and then take the first left onto Britton Street. Keep walking along Britton Street and the Jerusalem Tavern will soon come into view on the right hand side of the road.

LOCAL INFORMATION

The Jerusalem Tavern is the only pub in London that is owned and managed by St. Peter's Brewery from Bungay in Suffolk. Their brewery is inside a listed former agricultural building, and is a beautiful place to visit if you're ever down that way, but do book in advance if you want a tour.

Back in London, The Jerusalem Tavern is named after the Priory of St. John of Jerusalem, which was founded in 1140, and the tavern itself can be traced back to the 14th century. However, it has occupied several sites since then, before the current one.

If you want to know more about the Order of St. John, a museum can be found just around the corner that will tell you all about it. Turn left out of the pub, left on to Briset Street, and then left again when you reach St. John's Lane. The museum will be in front of you, set in a beautiful part of London that is worth visiting just for the view. It's almost like stepping back into medieval times.

St. John is, of course, where St. John's Ambulance takes its name from, and you can find them at the top of Briset Street.

55 Britton St, London EC1M 5UQ
Open: Mon-Fri 11am-11pm, Sun noon-6pm
Tel: 020 7490 4281
www.stpetersbrewery.co.uk/london-pub

DESCRIPTION

The building that is now home to The Jerusalem Tavern was developed in about 1720 and has been both a house and a shop over the years, and a pub since 1990. The shop front that now forms the exterior of the pub was added in the early part of the 19th century, while the interior of the pub is a largely wooden recreation of an 18th-century tavern.

They've made a great job of it. The floor is scuffed, the tables are marked and look suitably old, and everything does indeed look like it's been here for centuries. The pub is fairly small, with only a limited amount of seating available, although being on a side street means that the clientele can spill outside if it's all getting too busy indoors.

The beer on offer inevitably comes from St. Peter's Brewery. The beer is served from fake wooden casks that adorn the wall at the back of the bar, and when we were last in we had a half of Black IPA and a half of Honey Porter. Both were delicious, and served by friendly and knowledgeable staff. We had a chat about BrewDog beers with one person behind the bar, who clearly knew his stuff – always a good sign.

BREWDOG SHEPHERD'S BUSH

HOW TO GET THERE

This is a fine example of how the London Underground map, splendid creation though it is, can sometimes be misleading. The nearest tube station to the Shepherd's Bush branch of BrewDog is Goldhawk Road, and on the map it looks like Goldhawk Road and Shepherd's Bush underground lines are quite some distance apart. In reality, they're not, so if Shepherd's Bush suits you better then you won't have much further to walk to the pub.

Goldhawk Road is on the Hammersmith and City line, and also on a branch of the Circle line, but it will make your life a lot easier if you use the Hammersmith and City line (the pink one). This runs direct from places such as Hammersmith, Paddington, Baker Street, King's Cross and Liverpool Street, so you should be able to find a connection amongst all that lot.

If you take the Wells Road exit from the station you should turn left and walk until you reach Goldhawk Road, then turn right. If you take the Goldhawk Road exit, simply turn right. Either way, keep going along Goldhawk Road and BrewDog Shepherd's Bush will turn up on your right.

LOCAL INFORMATION

As a name, Shepherd's Bush sounds like it ought to have a bit of history behind it, and indeed it does. Unfortunately, there is very little in the way of concrete facts, and most of it is speculation. The most common theory is that it was used as a pasture for shepherds who were taking their sheep to Smithfield Market in the centre of London. Most of the land hereabouts would have been common ground, and it was still pretty much open farmland up until the end of the 19th century, when large scale residential development began to eat into the land.

All that remains now is the 8 acres of Shepherd's Bush Green, a triangular section of parkland with a pleasing number of trees.

As you leave the tube station you can't fail to notice Shepherd's Bush Market on the opposite side of the road, a street market with a whole host of items for sale and well worth a browse if you have the time.

15-19 Goldhawk Rd, London W12 8QQ
Open: Mon-Sat noon-midnight, Sun noon-10.30pm
Tel: 020 8749 8094
https://www.brewdog.com/bars/uk/shepherds-bush

DESCRIPTION

Don't let all the stories of super strong beers from BrewDog put you off visiting the place. Yes, they might have brewed a beer that was 55% ABV, and the 32% Tactical Nuclear Penguin is the best strong beer that we've ever tasted, but our default beer is the 3.8% Dead Pony Club, and that's what we had on our last visit. It's a lovely drink, crisp, refreshing, with a tropically hoppy taste to it.

This particular branch of the BrewDog chain opened in 2013 so it's a relative newcomer to the London beer scene. It is typically BrewDog in design, being robust and industrial in appearance, with a large menu of the available beers visible on a big display behind the bar.

The bar staff is very knowledgeable, as is usually the case with BrewDog bars, and even though it was very busy on a recent Thursday night visit, service was prompt. BrewDog bars never seem like the kind of place that you'd have as your local pub. On the other hand, they make excellent places to visit and while away an hour or two, and you'll almost always see a beer that you haven't had before.

THE FLASK

HOW TO GET THERE

The nearest tube station to The Flask is Hampstead, and it is very close indeed. It shouldn't take you more than a couple of minutes to find the pub.

Hampstead is on the Northern line and so gives easy access from many central London destinations, but you'll have to make sure that you're travelling north on the Edgware branch rather than the High Barnet or Mill Hill East branches. If the overhead displays are only showing the latter two destinations, take the first tube that turns up and change at Camden Town.

When you get off the train at Hampstead, enterprising souls can walk the 320 or so steps up a spiral staircase to get to ground level. The rest of us take one of the lifts.

Leaving by the main entrance, you'll need to turn left and walk down Hampstead High Street. The first turning on the left is Flask Walk, and as well as the pub that bears its name, it is home to an eclectic collection of shops. Linger by all means, but try to save some money for the pub, which is about 200 feet along Flask Walk on the right.

LOCAL INFORMATION

A lot of people come here simply to go for a walk on Hampstead Heath, and who can blame them? If you want to join them, you should leave the tube station and turn right and then almost immediately right again to find yourself on Heath Street. Stroll along until you reach a roundabout, and follow the road on the right. You'll soon be in the heart of the heath, and as the vast majority of it is open to the public, feel free to plunge in anywhere that takes your fancy.

Hampstead Heath is vast, covering almost 800 acres. There are records of it going back over 1,000 years. It's even mentioned in the Domesday Book. The green area to the left of what was Heath Street is called Golders Hill Park, and it has a deer enclosure and a small zoo (expect lemurs), along with several surprises like statues of dinosaurs, which can take the unwary (i.e. us) by surprise.

14 Flask Walk, London NW3 1HE
Open: Mon-Thu 11am-11pm, Fri-Sat 11am-midnight, Sun noon-10.30pm
Food: Mon-Thu 11am-10pm, Fri-Sat 11am-10pm Sun noon-9pm
Tel: 020 7435 4580
www.theflaskhampstead.co.uk

DESCRIPTION

As befits a Grade II listed building, there are some fine tiles to be seen on the walls outside The Flask. Step inside and you'll find a rather grand bar area that is split into four distinct sections. There's a public bar and a separate saloon bar at the front. There are some fine features here, including the wood and glass screen that helps to separate the two bars.

At the back of the pub there's a conservatory, and prior to that a fairly modern dining room. The pub has been in the hands of Young's brewery since 1904, so expect their full range of beers. It's more down to earth than the nearby Holly Bush pub that is described elsewhere in this book, and always makes us feel welcome. As usual on our most recent visit, we found ourselves drawn towards two pints of Young's Special.

We were in this pub one evening, enjoying a pint of that very beer, and had seen a couple in their late twenties enjoying a meal at the next table. Suddenly, without any words being exchanged, the chap tidied up all his belongings, got up, and walked out of the pub, leaving his partner staring after him open-mouthed in shock. When she noticed that we'd observed their little drama, she said to us slowly: 'awkward'. We never did find out what had happened.

THE HOLLY BUSH

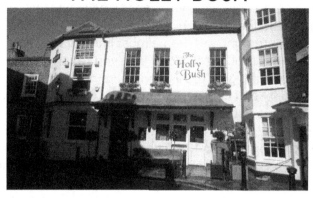

HOW TO GET THERE

The Holly Bush is in Hampstead on a branch of the Northern line. Make sure you're on the right branch because it splits into two sections at Camden Town. You want the Edgware branch line, so ignore the High Barnet or Mill Hill East trains. If you're south of Camden you can take one of these but change to the Edgware line at Camden.

Tube trivia: Hampstead is the deepest platform on the underground network, so unless you want to climb up a spiral staircase with over 320 steps, it makes more sense to take one of the lifts.

Leaving by the main exit, turn right and walk to a crossroads. On the wall opposite you is a sign saying Heath Street. Occasionally another exit is open, and that one is directly opposite the Heath Street sign so the directions from now on are the same either way.

Cross over the road. Holly Hill is the street to your left, so take a couple of paces towards it and turn right to walk up it. You'll soon find a narrow street with a sign on one side saying Holly Mount and one on the other side saying Holly Bush Hill. Turn right into this street, and the pub is on your left.

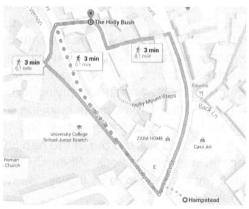

LOCAL INFORMATION
Apart from the pubs, the chief attraction around here is Hampstead
Heath. If you want to explore, follow Heath Street until you reach a
roundabout, then take the right fork in the road and go into the Heath
at any point that catches your eye. Keep walking long enough without
leaving the road and you'll come to a pub called The Spaniards Inn, which
Google describes as a 'rambling 16th-century inn', which seems about
right.

22 Holly Mount, London NW3 6SG
Open: Mon-Sat noon-11pm, Sun noon-10.30pm
Food: Mon-Fri noon-3pm and 6pm-10pm, Sat noon-4pm and 6pm-10pm,
Sun noon-5pm and 6pm-9pm
Tel: 020 7435 2892
www.hollybushhampstead.co.uk

DESCRIPTION
This Grade II listed building is now operated by Fuller's and was originally
a private house, built in the 1790s for the portrait painter George
Romney. He'd probably still recognise the interior today. It's a truly
delightful old pub, cosy and charming, nestling in a mews that positively
oozes wealth. It has several wood-panelled rooms to sit in, and etched
windows to admire, although it is the bar area itself that attracts the most
attention. The panelled bar counter is not the only survivor from Victorian
days, but it certainly catches the eye.

There are a couple of rooms available for private hire, one upstairs
and one downstairs. On one visit there, sitting near the bar with a pint of
London Pride, we watched an aristocratic lady of a certain age glide
through the bar and in a rather upper-class voice say to nobody in
particular: 'I assume we're in the Lady Hamilton Room'. So now you know
what one of the rooms is called (the other, upstairs one, is the Romney
Room).

The pub can get very busy, although there are outside areas
acting as an overspill. On our last visit on a Sunday lunchtime, around ten
camera (as opposed to CAMRA) enthusiasts came in and started taking
pictures of various items like candles, plants, cups of coffee and so on,
discussing it all with earnest enthusiasm. You might want to take a few
pictures yourself, as a reminder of a trip to a beautiful old pub.

THE HOLBORN WHIPPET

HOW TO GET THERE

As you might expect, the nearest station to The Holborn Whippet is indeed Holborn. This is on both the Central line and the Piccadilly line (tube trivia: it's the only station on the underground network where you can change between the two), and so should be an easy one to find, with direct connections from many well-known parts of London.

If you leave the station by the exit-only exit, which is to the right at the top of the last escalator, then you should see a sign for High Holborn on the wall on the far side of the road. Cross over the road at the traffic lights. Turn left and cross over the road again, and as soon as you've made it to the other side turn immediately right and proceed along Southampton Row.

If you leave the station by the main exit, you'll need to cross over the road in front of you, turn right, cross over High Holborn, and you'll now be on Southampton Row and heading in the right direction.

After only a minute or two you'll see a Victorian avenue of shops, cafes and various other stores on the left. This is Sicilian Avenue, and The Holborn Whippet is at the end on the left.

LOCAL INFORMATION

There's plenty to see and do around here. If you have a couple of hours to spare, head for the British Museum. It contains a wealth of material from all over the world, bringing human history to life. It's on Great Russell Street, and should be easy to find as there are plenty of maps on display on pillars in this part of London. And do you know what? It's free.

On a smaller scale, but no less fascinating for that, is the nearby Cartoon Museum on Little Russell Street. This covers the history of British cartoons and comic art from the 18th century to the present day.

If you like your museums to be a little more eccentric, try the Sir John Soane's Museum at 13 Lincoln's Inn Fields. It's in a 19th-century townhouse, former home of Sir John himself. He was one of the great English architects and the museum houses his own collection of antiques, paintings, sculptures, and more.

If you do visit Sir John's house, you should explore Lincoln's Inn Fields as well. It's the largest public square in London. Lincoln's Inn itself is one of the four inns of courts, where barristers are called to the bar. After all this exploration, you might feel the bar calling to you too.

25-29 Sicilian Ave, London WC1A 2QH
Open: Mon-Sat noon-11.30pm, Sun noon-10.30pm
Food: Daily noon-4pm and 5pm-9.30pm
Tel: 020 3137 9937
http://holbornwhippet.com

DESCRIPTION

So, why is it called The Holborn Whippet? Allegedly, the good people of Holborn and nearby Bloomsbury used to indulge in whippet racing in the 1800s, and then go for a drink afterwards. A likely story. Well, we can't do the whippet racing, but we can still have a drink.

The pub interior is vaguely retro in style, and the walls are adorned with some quirky prints. The seating, indeed the whole place, is functional rather than decorative, with plenty of wood on display on the bar, the floor, tables and bar stools.

But we're here for the beer, and the site of all those pumps on the wall behind the bar is what brought us. Helpful blackboards above the pumps tell you what's on, and rather obligingly they tell you a little bit about the style of the beer, as well as the usual information about name, strength and price. Of the many beers on offer on a recent visit, Northern Monk's Eternal IPA, often found in cans but available here on draught, was excellent and delightfully thirst-quenching on a warm, sunny day.

THE PRINCESS LOUISE

HOW TO GET THERE

The Princess Louise is served by Holborn tube station on the Central and Piccadilly lines. Plenty of popular areas of London connect up to one or the other of those lines, and if you're not on either of them then Leicester Square or King's Cross would be a good place to change to the Piccadilly line, or Oxford Circus on the Central line.

 The walk from tube to pub is one of the shorter ones in this book. Leave Holborn by the main exit, which is the one directly ahead of you when you come to the top of the escalators. Once you're on the pavement, turn right to the junction and a set of traffic lights. Turn left and cross over the road, and carry on walking along the road that you are now on, namely High Holborn, and the pub is on your left.

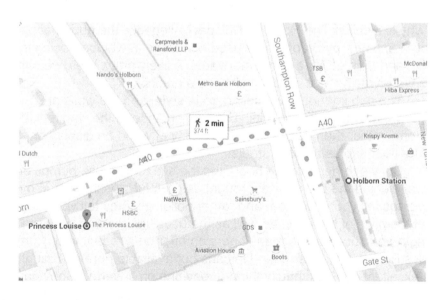

LOCAL INFORMATION

We first hear of the Holborn area way back in the 10th century, and like anywhere it has seen enormous changes in the last thousand years or so. In place of what would once have been open fields, you're now not too far from Covent Garden and its wealth of theatres, but also close to places like the British Museum.

The museum was founded in 1753, and quotes its oldest object as being a stone chopping tool dating back almost two million years. And with an estimated eight million objects in its collection, it should keep you busy for a while. Best of all, it won't cost you a penny to get in. You might spend plenty of money when you get inside though, as their four shops could inspire a few unusual Christmas presents.

208 High Holborn, London WC1V 7EP
Open: Mon-Fri 11am-11pm, Sat noon-11pm, Sun noon-6.45pm
Food: Mon-Thu noon-2.30pm and 6pm-8.30pm, Fri noon-2.30pm
Tel: 020 7405 8816
http://princesslouisepub.co.uk

DESCRIPTION

The Grade II listed Princess Louise first opened its doors to the public in the early 1870s, and is named after Princess Louise, Duchess of Argyll, sixth child and fourth daughter of Queen Victoria and Prince Albert.

There was a remodelling of the pub as recently as 1891, and a later, very sympathetic, rework in 2007. This restored the pub to be more like the original version, even bringing back the glass-walled cubicles that the Victorians admired so much.

The interior of the pub is a true gem. Plenty of multi-coloured tile work? Check. Mahogany bar top? Check. Large, ornate mirrors? Check. It probably looked very similar in its Victorian days, and it's a joy that this time capsule is still with us today. Not for nothing has it been referred to as a 'national treasure'.

The pub is run and maintained by the Samuel Smith brewery, who deserve a pat on the back for the state of the pub. Their Old Brewery bitter, served here in cask form when we were last at the bar, is remarkably cheap for a pub in this part of London. Well, anywhere in London, come to that. Just check the service charge first if you're going to pay by credit card. It's not cheap.

THE GRENADIER

HOW TO GET THERE

The nearest tube station for The Grenadier is Hyde Park Corner, probably the most confusing tube station on the entire network to get into and out of. It's on the Piccadilly line only, so you might find yourself changing at the likes of Earl's Court, Leicester Square or King's Cross before getting here. When you do make it, take exit 4 from the station. This will lead you to the south side of Knightsbridge, and when you exit you should carry on walking ahead of you along the south side of Knightsbridge.

Look for the very narrow street on your left, Old Barrack Yard, which is where things can get confusing as it twists around. Walk down Old Barrack Yard and past Wilton Place on your right. Just beyond here Old Barrack Yard does a very sharp right, which you take. At the end turn right and you'll find The Grenadier on your right. A wooden door leads you to the front of the pub where there's a rather splendid red sentry box. We advise not drinking too much at The Grenadier as you'll never find your way out again.

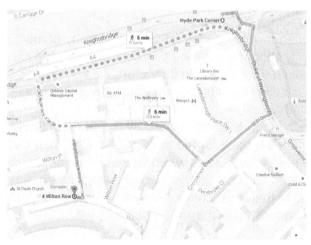

LOCAL INFORMATION

As its name implies, Hyde Park Corner is indeed in a corner of Hyde Park, tucked away in the south-east. It might equally be called Green Park Corner, because it's at the north-western end of that particular park too, so you've got two extensive sets of parkland to explore if the weather's fair and you've got the time to spare.

If you've got even more time, Apsley House is near to the tube station. It's a grand old house that was home to the Duke of Wellington in the 19th century (the Iron Duke, as he was nicknamed), and carried the address Number One, London. Nowadays it's at 149 Piccadilly, which sounds nowhere near as imposing. It's a museum now, with an extensive art collection, and you'll be stunned as you walk around the interior of this palatial residence. You can't believe that anybody could live in such splendour, but the Duke of Wellington once did.

Indeed, the current Duke still lives here. Although most of the house was given to the nation by the 7th Duke in the 1940s, the family still retain the right to live in around half of it as long as there remains a Duke of Wellington.

18 Wilton Row, Belgrave Square, London SW1X 7NR
Open: Daily noon-11pm
Food: Daily noon-10pm
Tel: 020 7235 3074
www.taylor-walker.co.uk/pub/grenadier-belgrave-square/c0800

DESCRIPTION

The Grenadier takes great pride in allegedly being haunted, and proclaims itself to be 'The UK's most haunted pub!' The ghost that does the haunting is meant to be that of a young grenadier who had been caught cheating at cards. His comrades were so incensed at this that they beat him to death, and the ghost – nicknamed Cedric – is said to be most prominent around the month of September.

One thing you can't fail to notice inside the pub is the huge collection of signed bank notes attached to the ceiling. There are hundreds of them! They're meant to be used for paying off the debts of Cedric the ghost, but it's probably a bit late for that now, no matter which pub he ended his days in.

It's an old pub, nice and quirky (there's a notice that says only people arriving by taxi or on foot will get served), and slightly expensive even for this area, but we enjoyed ourselves on a recent visit so it's worth it. We had a decent conversation with two bar staff about the music of the Saw Doctors, spent some time reading up the history of the Grenadier Guards from a series of prints on the walls, and found our pints of Abbott Ale to be in top class condition.

OAKA AT THE MANSION HOUSE

Photo courtesy of Oaka at the Mansion House

HOW TO GET THERE

The awkwardly named Oaka at the Mansion House (all will be revealed) has Kennington as its nearest tube station, and it's very near indeed.

Kennington is on the Northern line, and is the first stop south from where the two separate branches of that line travel across central London. Therefore, if you're travelling from anywhere north of Kennington, simply take the first tube that turns up and don't worry about which branch of the line it's going to be travelling along. It'll take you seven stops to get from Euston to Kennington on the Charing Cross branch, or nine if you're going via Bank.

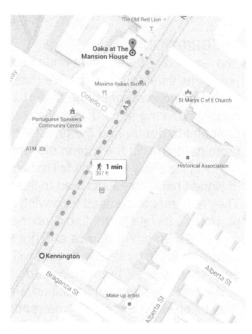

The same applies if you're travelling north to Kennington from the likes of Clapham or Tooting: all Northern line trains go through Kennington.

The exit from Kennington tube station will place you at the junction of Braganza Street off to the left, and Kennington Park Road to the right. The best bet for getting to the pub is to cross over Kennington Park Road as soon as you come out of the tube station, and then turn right. In less than a minute, you'll see the pub on your left hand side.

LOCAL INFORMATION

There's something of a Shakespearean thing going on around here, as we noticed an Othello Close, Falstaff Court, and Portia and Hamlet Courts as well. Although we've no idea why these streets should be named in this manner, we can tell you that the 'Oaka' part of 'Oaka at the Mansion House' is referring to a brewery called Oakham Ales, who are based in Peterborough. When Oakham were looking for a dedicated London pub to showcase their beers, they settled on the Mansion House, which is still the name displayed above the door outside the pub.

Apart from the pub, Kennington is also home to The Oval cricket ground, although if you're going there then Oval is the nearest underground station, not Kennington. Between Oval and Kennington tube stations you'll find Kennington Park, a place where they used to hold public executions. The last one was in 1800, so no need to worry.

The last remaining major point of interest before we turn back to the pub is the Imperial War Museum, which should take about 15 minutes to reach on foot from Kennington tube station.

48 Kennington Park Rd, London SE11 4RS
Open: Sun-Thu noon-midnight, Fri-Sat noon-late
Food: Mon-Fri noon-2.30pm and 5.30pm-10.30pm, Sat noon-3.30pm and 5.30pm-10.30pm, Sun noon-3.30pm and 5.30pm-10pm
Tel: 020 7582 5599
www.oakalondon.com

DESCRIPTION

If you like cask beer and Pan-Asian food, and appreciate a modern pub with a dining room, then you've come to the right place. Just because it features Oakham ales doesn't mean that it's Oakham-exclusive. They sell quite a range of beers from different breweries, in various cask, keg and bottled varieties.

A lot of the brews are from local breweries, but we settled on two pints of Chemical Syndicate, feeling that if Oakham can go to the effort of getting their beer from Peterborough to London, we should go to the effort of carrying it from bar to mouth. Chemical Syndicate is a five-hopped golden ale, with a touch of sweetness about it, and it kept making us both think of caramel, which isn't a bad thing at all.

The pub itself is pretty contemporary, comfortable, with the metal bottom of a mash tun beneath your feet when you enter, and a rather unusual water feature on the wall. There are a few tables out at the front if the weather is up to it, and while the front and right area of the place functions mainly as a pub, its principal focus in the rest of the building is definitely on food.

THE PINEAPPLE

HOW TO GET THERE

The nearest tube station to The Pineapple is Kentish Town on the High Barnet branch of the Northern line, and is easy enough to find as long as you make the correct turn out of the exit.

      The Northern line serves a number of important mainline stations, such as Euston, King's Cross, Charing Cross and Waterloo. If you're standing on the platform and the monitors are stubbornly displaying tubes going to Edgware for the foreseeable future, simply get one of those and change to a High Barnet tube at Camden.

      When you leave the station, turn immediately right and walk a short distance to point yourself at The Assembly Room pub on the other side of Leighton Road. Cross over Leighton Road and turn right, then take the first left, which will be Leverton Street. Then it's just a case of keeping going until you get to the pub, passing Falkland Road along the way. The pub is on the corner of Leverton Street and Ascham Street.

LOCAL INFORMATION

Kentish Town first appears in the history books in 1207, when it was known as Kentisston. By the mid-15th century it was a growing village, and gradually became absorbed into London as all the towns and villages grew in size and spread out to become what is essentially one large sprawling metropolis.

Nevertheless, walking around the place does give you a sense that Kentish Town still sees itself as a village within London. Pubs like The Pineapple enhance that feeling.

If you're feeling particularly bold, you could turn left out of the tube station and spend three minutes walking down Kentish Town Road until you see a place called Rio's on the opposite side from the exit. It describes itself as Rio's Relaxation Spa, or in other words, a home to people who like to bathe in the nuddy, and preferably in company. Personally, we're going to the pub...

51 Leverton St, London NW5 2NX
Open: Mon-Sat noon-11.30pm, Sun noon-11pm
Tel: 020 7284 4631
https://www.facebook.com/ThePineapplePub

DESCRIPTION

We nearly lost The Pineapple at the start of this century, which would have been a huge shame. It had been threatened with closure and being converted into flats, but a high-profile media campaign achieved the near impossible and got it a Grade II English Heritage status in just eight days.

The pub first opened in 1868 to serve the thirsty needs of the rail workers who had invaded the area. It's much bigger than it appears from the outside, and its quirky charm is visible the moment you step in. If you can tear your attention away from the numerous hand pumps and look behind the bar, you'll see some fine etched mirrors. There's also plenty of interesting memorabilia from the campaign to save the pub from closure.

There are corridors full of comfy seating to either side of the bar, leading into a relatively new conservatory and a garden. There's also a small seating area at the front. It needs all this space because it can get very busy, especially if there's a concert on at the nearby O2 Forum, or it's one of the pub's many themed nights (quiz, comedy, music etc). Or it's busy simply because it's a very fine pub. There was a beer festival on when we were last there, and our pints of Milk Stout from the Bristol Beer Factory were particularly good, with chocolate and coffee notes alongside the subtle milky lactose taste.

Together with the nearby Southampton Arms, The Pineapple makes Kentish Town a must-visit place for any discerning drinker.

THE SOUTHAMPTON ARMS

Photo (c) Helen Cathcart

HOW TO GET THERE

Tufnell Park is just about the closest tube station to The Southampton Arms, but it's not the easiest of routes from tube to pub, as we discovered once. Ever since, we've always approached the pub from Kentish Town station instead, and as Tufnell Park was closed when we were last there, and there's only a minute or so in it anyway, we'll do the same now.

Kentish Town is on the Northern line, and you'll have to make sure that you're on a tube that's heading for either High Barnet or Mill Hill East. If the overhead displays are only advertising tubes for Edgware Road, take the first one that turns up and change to the other branch line at Camden Town.

When you leave the exit, there'll be a crossroads pretty much in front of you. Leighton Road will be heading off to the right, with a pub called The Assembly House on one corner. Worth a detour. For now, though, cross over Leighton Road, and walk north along Kentish Town Road. You'll soon come to a fork in the road. Take the left fork, Highgate Road, for about five minutes until you go under a railway bridge, and then The Southampton Arms will appear on the left.

LOCAL INFORMATION

Before venturing out here, if you can it is well worth consulting the website for the O2 Forum in Kentish Town (www.o2forumkentishtown.co.uk). The Forum is a music venue inside a large former cinema, and you'll pass it just after the fork of Fortess Road and Highgate Road. If there's an event on at the Forum, pubs in the local area can get very busy indeed, so you might want to visit at lunchtime or wait until they haven't scheduled any concerts.

If you do come visiting, there are three pubs in this book which are relatively close together here, and they form a nice little circuit. There's The Southampton Arms itself, The Pineapple, and The Junction Tavern. The latter is a 3-minute stroll along Fortess Road from Tufnell Park tube station.

If you're a lover of a style of music known as pub rock, you should pause outside the Forum and cast your eyes over to the other side of the road. That is where a pub called the Tally Ho used to stand, and it's where pub rock really started, with people like Ian Dury, Joe Strummer, Nick Lowe, Dr Feelgood and many others, all putting in appearances. Alas, the pub is no more.

139 Highgate Rd, London NW5 1LE
Open: Daily noon-11pm, sometimes later
Tel: None
www.thesouthamptonarms.co.uk

DESCRIPTION

The Southampton Arms first opened its doors in 2009. A fine sign outside advertises it as an Ale and Cider House, and it has a large number of beer pumps on the front of the bar and cider dispensed from the back.

At first glance the pub looks like it's been around for some time, with a large mirror and several fine prints on the wall to the left, a couple of padded seating areas off to your right, and several tables and benches by the side of the wall in front of you. This leaves a narrow gap between the bar and the people sitting near the wall, and it gets more crowded further down as you head towards the toilets and a small beer garden, because there's a piano squeezed in as well.

The piano isn't in use all the time, but on our first visit there was somebody playing away. We had to smile when they started playing Roll out the Barrel, thinking here we are in a London boozer living a cliché right now, but then that segued into Stairway To Heaven before going out with Fats Domino's Blueberry Hill. The piano player received a richly deserved round of applause. Memories like that help to make this one of our favourite London pubs.

THE BETJEMAN ARMS

HOW TO GET THERE

Your nearest underground station to The Betjeman Arms is King's Cross, which means the Northern line (Bank branch), Piccadilly, Victoria, Circle, Metropolitan, and Hammersmith and City lines all go through here.

Having said that, it can start to get difficult when you are leaving the underground station, as there are so many exits to choose from. If you spy one with Pancras Road written on it, head towards it, but otherwise just follow signs saying 'St Pancras International' and aim towards ground level.

Once you reach the surface, you'll need to locate St Pancras International Station, which is on the opposite side of Pancras Road from King's Cross station. This enormous Grade 1 listed building first opened in 1868, and was narrowly saved from demolition in the early 1960s.

If you were to stand on nearby Euston Road and look across it at St Pancras station and the adjoining hotel, the Betjeman Arms is tucked away in the bottom right hand corner. There are steps leading up to the pub from Pancras Road, with the pub on the right once you get to the top, or you can approach it from the front of the hotel. This follows a sloping driveway that curves around to the right, and in this instance you'll find the pub on your left.

LOCAL INFORMATION

The pub is named in honour of Sir John Betjeman, who was at the forefront of the campaign that saved the station from being demolished in the 1960s. Inside the station there's a large statue of Sir John in a rather striking pose. It's not the only statue in the station. If you wander out on to the station concourse at the back of the pub, you'll see a 9-metre tall statue called The Meeting Place, meant to represent a random couple meeting up at the station. The frieze that runs beneath it bears close examination, as it is full of fascinating detail.

Stroll around the station and you'll see several pianos waiting to be played by anyone who cares to tickle the ivories. One was donated to the station by Sir Elton John. He signed it following a public performance at the station in February 2016.

Among the many other marvels in the station, you should keep an eye out for the Dent Clock. It hangs above the couple in The Meeting Place statue, and was made by a company founded by Edward John Dent in 1814. They won the contract to supply the clock to the Parliament at Westminster, which normally gets called Big Ben, although Big Ben refers to the Great Bell inside the clock tower, rather than the clock itself.

53 St Pancras International Station, London N1C 4QL
Open: Mon-Sat 8am-11pm, Sun 9am-10.30pm
Food: Mon-Sat 8am-9.30pm, Sun 9am-9pm
Tel: 020 7923 5440
www.thebetjemanarms.co.uk

DESCRIPTION

This claims to be the last pub before Paris, which makes sense when you consider that this is where you catch the Eurostar trains to Paris. Monitors hang in the bar to give you a live feed of train departures. The main bar is quite an open area, with separate rooms beyond it for dining, and it usually just has the three beers on cask. We often plump for their house Betjeman Ale, which is the same beer as Cornish Coaster from Sharp's Brewery over in Devon. It's a pleasant enough golden ale without being spectacular.

The beauty of it, though, is that you can take it outside to the back of the pub, and sit and watch the trains coming in and out of the station. There's a separate bar out here, although it isn't always manned.

From here you can see The Meeting Place statue, the Dent Clock and you might even see a hawk. One has been hired to scare away the pigeons, and it certainly works. We've never seen a pigeon inside here. Mind you, the hawk almost scared us away as it flew right by our heads when we saw it for the first time!

THE PARCEL YARD

HOW TO GET THERE

The Grade I listed building that is the Parcel Yard pub lies to one end of the main station concourse at King's Cross, and so King's Cross underground station is your target for this one. The station is on the Northern (Bank branch), Victoria, Piccadilly, Hammersmith and City, Metropolitan and Circle lines, which should give you plenty of options for getting here.

There are numerous exits from King's Cross underground station, and it would take several pages to describe them all. Aim for the National Rail Departures Concourse rather any of the outside exits, because you don't need to leave the station to find the pub.

When you get to the concourse, you should be looking for the train departure boards high above your head. Once you've found those, you'll see the Harry Potter shop to the left of them at platform nine and three-quarters. There's usually quite a queue of people outside it waiting to get their picture taken, and they provide endless amusement if you're sitting outside the pub watching them, because the pub is just to the left of the shop and up a flight of steps. There's also a lift, if the steps prove problematic for any reason.

LOCAL INFORMATION

Despite lacking the architectural grandeur of its near-neighbour St. Pancras International, King's Cross is still quite a striking building in its own right. For years it was dark, old and distinctly gloomy, but a refurbishment that seems to have lasted for decades has finally resulted in this part of London getting the decent station that its growing gentrification deserves.

The revamped station at King's Cross is now light, bright, very airy, has plenty of room inside, and has an eye-catching ceiling display that will have you itching to take a picture of it.

There are now plenty of shops on the main concourse. Not as many as St. Pancras, granted, but sufficient for most needs. Most of the familiar ones are here, and as it's on the way from the front of the station to the Parcel Yard, the Pasty Shop in particular is a difficult one to walk past without calling for a bite to eat.

However, you could always wait until you get to the pub, because food plays a big part in the life of the Parcel Yard (they start serving breakfast at 8am). And, we are delighted to say, so does beer.

> Kings Cross Station, London N1 9AL
> Mon-Sat 8am-11pm, Sun 9am-10.30pm
> Food: Mon-Sat 8am-10pm, Sun 9am-9pm
> Tel: 020 7713 7258
> www.parcelyard.co.uk

DESCRIPTION

Once a parcels office back in 1852, this has been splendidly brought back to life by Fuller's, and in many ways it reflects the station itself. It's open, bright and makes great use of glass (see the central atrium and its glass ceiling). Unlike the station, it has a wooden floor, which only adds to the charm. The bar is on two levels, with upstairs being predominantly food-led, while the downstairs level is where most of the drinking goes on. As you might imagine, it can attract huge crowds as the homeward commute commences in the evening, so you might prefer to get there mid-afternoon, or wait until the weekend.

It's a big pub, though, with several different drinking areas downstairs. A straight corridor from the front door will take you through to the impressive bar, and there were almost 30 cask and keg offerings on a recent visit. There's also a small terrace outside the front door, from where you can observe the line of fans outside the Harry Potter shop.

The beers in the Parcel Yard are predominantly Fuller's and cover a wide range of drinks (ESB for us, thanks), although guests do crop up on a frequent basis. Their prices aren't the cheapest in London but we fully support them if it means buildings like this can continue to operate.

THE QUEEN'S HEAD

HOW TO GET THERE

King's Cross is handy for The Queen's Head and it's served by no fewer than six different lines: Hammersmith and City, Circle, Metropolitan, Northern, Piccadilly and Victoria.

Things start to get a little bit confusing when it comes to leaving the station, because there are plenty of different exits. You're looking for the south side of Euston Road, and even here there are two exits to choose from. You want to be standing outside King's Cross Post Office when you get to the surface, but don't worry if you come up outside Barclays Bank. Just orient yourself so that King's Cross and St Pancras are on your left, and start walking along Euston Road. You'll reach the Post Office in no time. Just check the map to get your orientation.

Keep walking along Euston Road, with King's Cross on your left. The road will shortly veer off to the right, and you need to veer off with it. This takes you into Gray's Inn Road, so follow that past Britannia Street and Swinton Street then turn left into Acton Street. The pub is a short way down, on the left.

LOCAL INFORMATION
While you're in the area, it would be a shame to miss the chance to take a look at Percy Circus. Reaching it is simple enough. Walk past the Queen's Head (temporarily, of course) and keep going along Acton Street. When the road splits, cross over onto Great Percy Street, and Percy Circus is at the end of that street.

Percy Circus consists of an open garden area surrounded by trees, with some more trees in the middle, and a circular railing running around it. Work started on it in 1841, although it took another twelve years before it reached completion. It has been described as 'one of the most delightful bits of town planning in London'. It is indeed very pleasant to look at and walk around, or through, and it should be viewed while it still survives, as there are very few of these circuses left in London.

66 Acton St, London WC1X 9NB
Open: Sun-Mon noon-11pm, Tue-Sat noon-midnight
Tel: 020 7713 5772
http://queensheadlondon.com

DESCRIPTION
Having worked up a thirst, let's return to The Queen's Head. Unprepossessing and unpromising to look at from the outside, even though the large bay window lends a certain amount of charm, things soon improve when you step inside.

There are some comfortable settees (which can be difficult to get out of!) arranged about the single bar, and a number of wooden chairs and tables make it rather easier to reach your food or drink without the great effort of rising from a settee.

Decorative mirrors opposite the bar make the place look bigger than it really is, and it's all quite comfortable. We found it delightful. Music is something of a feature here, as you might guess from the well-maintained piano on your right as you walk in, as – naturally – is beer.

There are normally three cask ales on, along with a number of keg and bottled offerings. If you're very lucky, they might have one of their own beers on, as this is a brewpub and they have a small brewery in the cellar. We missed out last time, but had a decent pint from Revolutions Brewing Company called Kissing with Confidence. No need to make a joke about the name as the bar staff have heard them all before.

THE SOURCED MARKET

Photo courtesy of The Sourced Market

HOW TO GET THERE

This can be a confusing one to find first (or second, or third) time around, so we'll start with the easy bit and say that you've got to get to King's Cross station before heading out into the open air. The Northern, Victoria, Piccadilly, Hammersmith and City, Metropolitan and Circle lines all go through here, which should make it relatively straightforward to get to, wherever you are in London.

When you arrive at King's Cross, follow exit signs pointing you towards St. Pancras International, because The Sourced Market is inside that station. Now the fun begins.

Wherever you emerge from King's Cross, as long as you've followed directions for St. Pancras International you should be standing on Pancras Road. Cross over the road, start walking to your right, and find the first entrance to St. Pancras International that you can. Now you need to follow signs directing you to National Rail Tickets. The Sourced Market is opposite the ticket office. And it's not a pub. More of that later.

LOCAL INFORMATION

The outside of St. Pancras International is magnificent, and it's hard to believe that it almost got knocked down in the 1960s. This provoked outrage in many quarters, and a campaign led by future poet laureate Sir John Betjeman eventually won the day and the building was saved. It is now a Grade I listed building, and so this wonderful example of Victorian architecture is safe for the foreseeable future. In honour of the work that Sir John Betjeman put in during the campaign, there's a statue of the great man in typical pose upstairs inside the station.

Just around the corner from St. Pancras, across Midland Road, stands the British Library. This too is a Grade I listed building, and in terms of number of items catalogued, it is the largest library in the world. It might keep you occupied for a while, but if you're getting thirsty and want to get to The Sourced Market, follow us.

St Pancras International, Pancras Road, London NW1 2QP
Open: Mon-Fri 6.30am-9pm, Sat 7.30am-8pm, Sun 8.30am-8pm
Tel: 020 7183 3251
http://sourcedmarket.com

DESCRIPTION

We said earlier that The Sourced Market isn't a pub, and in the strictest sense of the term it isn't. However, you can drink alcohol here, so the rules for inclusion in this book got bent a little. It's a place we go to frequently, and it amply repays a visit. It opened in 2009 and, as its name implies, there's a lot more to it than beer. Coffee, cheese, fruit and vegetables, bread and much more, can all be bought here.

The beer can be found on several shelves and inside a fridge, located in a corner in the top right of the Market. London breweries are favoured here, but by no means exclusively, and you can buy bottles and cans to take away or to drink on the premises.

Although we've bought numerous bottles to take away here, we take great pleasure in buying a bottle, pouring it into a glass, and sitting down at one of the tables in front of the Market. There you can relax and watch people hurrying and scurrying about as they try to catch their train. As they rush about and panic, you take a measured sip of your drink, knowing that the only decision you've got to make is what to drink next.

THE NAGS HEAD

HOW TO GET THERE

The nearest stop for the Nags Head (without an apostrophe) is Knightsbridge, which is on the Piccadilly line and easily accessible from many parts of London. You need Exit 3. This puts you on Brompton Road, so turn right out of the station and follow the road as it changes its name to Knightsbridge.

The simplest route is to follow Knightsbridge until Wilton Place appears on the right. Turn right to walk down it until you reach Kinnerton Street, and turn right again. You'll soon reach a crossroads where Kinnerton Street has something of an identity crisis and appears to run in several different directions. A Shepherd Neame pub called The Wilton Arms is just over the crossroads in front of you and on the right, but you need to turn left and proceed down this branch of Kinnerton Street for a short distance until the pub appears on the right.

Don't look for the name Nags Head, though. What identifies it is the name of the long-serving landlord, Kevin Moran, in big letters on the front.

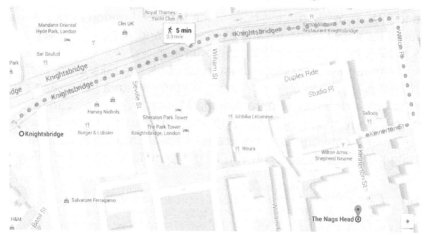

LOCAL INFORMATION

Interesting part of London, this, a fairly quiet corner of Knightsbridge and seemingly a long way away from the hustle and bustle of normal life in the city.

But as always, the city is never too far away. Chief amongst the nearby attractions is of course Hyde Park, although some might argue that it's Harvey Nichols. Hyde Park is easily reached from the tube station, just cross over the road when you reach ground level and keep going in a northerly direction. It's worth the walk. Hyde Park is one of the larger parks in London, although it's actually split into two separate areas, namely Hyde Park and Kensington Gardens.

The Grade 1 listed Kensington Gardens were separated from the rest of Hyde Park in 1728 at the request of Queen Caroline, queen to King George II's king. They're rather more formal than Hyde Park and, somewhat confusingly, have different opening hours. The Serpentine Bridge forms the boundary between the gardens and the park.

53 Kinnerton St, London SW1X 8ED
Open: Daily 11am-11pm
Tel: 020 7235 1135
Website: None

DESCRIPTION

Well, if ever a pub divided opinion, it's this one. Some Internet reviewers despise it, others love it, but personally we've never had less than a cordial greeting every time we've been in. Indeed, on our most recent visit, we ended up having a splendid chat with two of the bar staff about the music of The Saw Doctors and The Pogues. We also had a decent pint of Adnams Broadside.

The first time you walk into the pub you could easily think that you've stumbled into some kind of bizarre antique shop that just happens to have a very low bar counter in it (reputedly the lowest in London), as seemingly every square inch of wall space - and quite a lot of floor space come to that - is covered in a rather eccentric collection of bric-a-brac. There are many marvellous photographs to gaze at as you stroll around the small bar area with your drink. There's even a What the Butler Saw machine, and it's worth going into the pub just for that. It's probably best visited outside peak drinking hours because of the tiny size of the pub.

THE STAR TAVERN

Photo courtesy of The Star Tavern

HOW TO GET THERE

Knightsbridge underground station is your starting point for this one, and it's on the Piccadilly line. This is not the easiest of pubs to find, although it does reward the journey. At times you feel like you're trespassing on private property, but as far as we're aware, you're not.

Leave the tube station by Exit 3, which will place you on Brompton Road. Turn to the right and walk the short distance to Sloane Street, then turn right and carry on until you come to Harriet Street, at which point turn left. After a short distance you should turn right onto Lowndes Square, and after reaching the bottom end of a small grassy area you need to turn right onto Lowndes Street.

This is where it gets interesting. When you reach West Halkin Street, you should turn left and keep going until you reach Halkin Place and turn right, and then, feeling rather like a naughty schoolboy ignoring a No Trespassing sign, walk along Halkin Place and go straight ahead under the archway that appears in front of you. The pub is immediately on your right.

LOCAL INFORMATION

We started this journey at Knightsbridge tube station, and if you take the same tube exit but turn left on Sloane Street instead of turning right, you'll not only find another tube exit on the other side of the road, but you'll also find a path between two buildings that leads you the short distance to Hyde Park. A helpful map by the tube exit should point you in the right direction.

This is a detour well worth making. Hyde Park is one of the Royal Parks of London, and has a long history. It was created by Henry VIII in 1536, and he used it for hunting. We commoners had to wait until 1637 before we were allowed to use it.

There are many attractions to be found in the park, including the fabled Speakers' Corner, which is not far from where Tyburn Gallows used to stand. Less grisly is a very pleasant stroll around The Serpentine, a lake that dates back to 1730. Far more recent, and near the south side of The Serpentine, is the Diana Princess of Wales Memorial Fountain.

6 Belgrave Mews West, London SW1X 8HT
Open: Mon-Fri 11am-11pm, Sat noon-11pm, Sun noon-10.30pm
Food: Mon-Sat noon-3pm and 5pm-9pm, Sun noon-4pm and 5pm-9pm
Tel: 020 7235 3019
www.star-tavern-belgravia.co.uk

DESCRIPTION

We can take Pride in this Belgravia pub, because it's a Fuller's Brewery house with a good range of their beers, although there's usually a guest ale on as well. The pub is Grade II listed and was established in 1848, and you can see why it gets its listing: plenty of wood panelling, and to continue our schoolboy theme of earlier, you can be forgiven a snigger when you find the Thomas Crapper Wash Basins. Fans of pub quiz trivia will already know that the word 'crap' for, er, bodily waste is nothing to do with Thomas Crapper but goes back much further in history.

You're in the company of interesting ghosts here, as it was home to many a movie star in the 1950s and 1960s. It was also, allegedly, the place where the Great Train Robbers made their plans in 1963.

Fortunately, times change, and the pub now has a much friendlier clientele, and you might still see some of the rich and famous in this prosperous area. It's also another one where the chandelier fans can find plenty to enjoy. Not for nothing did The Telegraph newspaper vote it the best historical pub in Central London.

THE LAMB AND FLAG

Photo courtesy of The Lamb and Flag

HOW TO GET THERE

There are two tube stations pretty much equidistant from The Lamb and Flag, and these are Covent Garden and Leicester Square. Covent Garden is only served by the Piccadilly line, whereas Leicester Square links up with both the Piccadilly line and the Northern line (Charing Cross branch) so we'll go with Leicester Square.

Find the exit onto Cranbourn Street and when you emerge, turn left. Walk to the junction of several roads and cross over Cranbourn Street to your right. Cross over the next street at the junction too, which is St Martin's Lane. Cross over the next street as well, which is Garrick Street. Walk down Garrick Street on the left-hand side and past the cobblestone entrance to Floral Street on your left. Look carefully for the even smaller cobblestoned entrance to Rose Street, and turn left along here. Hoorah! The Lamb and Flag is in front of you.

LOCAL INFORMATION

What's in a name? Leicester Square is named after Robert Sidney, the 2nd Earl of Leicester, who bought the land in 1630 and by 1635 had built himself one of the grandest houses in London at the time, which he named Leicester House.

Our old acquaintance William Hogarth once lived here (the artist who painted, amongst many others, Gin Lane and Beer Street), as did another renowned artist Joshua Reynolds. Even the then Prince of Wales, Frederick, lived here for a brief time in 1742 and 1743.

The Square has changed much over the years, and gradually during the 18th and 19th centuries it began to be a home to all sorts of popular entertainment of the day, although we're a long way away from bear-baiting these days. Leicester Square continues to be a home to all manner of modern entertainment, and after some much needed pedestrianisation in the 1980s, it became a much safer place to walk around. And Leicester House, that started it all off? It was demolished at the end of the 18th century, and after a spell with a church in its place, the Prince Charles Cinema now stands on roughly the same spot as the original house.

33 Rose St, London WC2E 9EB
Open: Mon-Sat 11am-11pm, Sun noon-10.30pm
Food: Mon-Thu noon-8pm, Fri-Sat noon-5pm, Sun noon-9pm
Tel: 020 7497 9504
www.lambandflagcoventgarden.co.uk

DESCRIPTION

The first mention of a pub in this location was in 1772, although it was known as The Cooper's Arms until 1883. It's been called The Lamb and Flag ever since. It has a bloodthirsty past, staging bareknuckle fights in the 19th century, and acquired the nickname The Bucket of Blood, although it's all calmed down now.

The ground floor has a long and rather narrow bar, with some wonderfully ornate wooden panelling at the front of it. Wooden floors, oak beams and brass fittings abound, with a lamb and a flag etched into a glass window to the right of the bar. It gets very busy during peak times, and it's always been peak time whenever we've been in! In which case, head up the creaky stairs to the Dryden Room where you might find more space. The Dryden Room honours poet John Dryden, who was assaulted in the alleyway that runs alongside the pub by thugs hired by the then Earl of Rochester, with whom he had a bitter rivalry.

Today The Lamb and Flag is a nice combination of old and new, and feels comfortably lived in. With a pint of Oliver's Island in hand, gaze around and reflect on the history of this grand old building. And yes, Dickens did drink here!

THE LORD ABERCONWAY

HOW TO GET THERE

The nearest underground station to the Lord Aberconway is Liverpool Street, and if you head to the internet and look at this pub on a Google Maps page, you'll see the description 'rail station pub with mezzanine balcony'. From this, you would be forgiven for thinking that the pub is actually on Liverpool Street station somewhere. We certainly did, the first time we went. We were wrong.

So, first you'll need to get to Liverpool Street underground station, which is on the Metropolitan (magenta), Circle (yellow), Central (red) and Hammersmith and City (pink) lines. This gives you plenty of opportunities for getting here.

As you leave the underground station, head for Old Broad Street. If you find yourself crossing a road (Liverpool Street) and aiming towards the mainline station, turn around and come back. When you emerge from the underground station there should be a pub called The Railway more or less opposite you. Ignore this pub but turn left instead and The Lord Aberconway is just a few yards along. At the time of writing there is a lot of construction work going on around the station, so take care.

LOCAL INFORMATION

Liverpool Street Station, which opened in 1874, is reckoned to be the third busiest mainline train station in the country, with only Waterloo and Victoria carrying more passengers, thus putting three London stations at the top of the list.

The underground station followed in 1875, although the two only acquired their present name in 1909. Prior to that, they had been referred to by the name of an earlier station on the site, called Bishopgate. Incidentally, the pub's name hints at the railway connection, because it's named after a former chairman of the old Metropolitan Railway before it became merged into the London Passenger Transport Board.

Bishopgate station is long gone now (as is the London Passenger Transport Board), and if you want to pay homage to it then the railway station on Shoreditch High Street stands on roughly the same spot. However, that's about a 15-minute walk, and takes you much too far away from the pub.

72 Old Broad Street, London EC2M 1QT
Open: Mon-Fri 10am-11pm, Sat noon-10pm, Sun noon-6pm
Tel: 020 7929 1743
www.nicholsonspubs.co.uk/restaurants/london/thelordaberconwayliver-poolstreetlondon

DESCRIPTION

Another word that Google Maps uses to describe the Lord Aberconway is 'statuesque', and this time they're not wrong. The elegant dining area upstairs at mezzanine level is particularly appealing. This is only hinted at from the outside, where it looks like a decidedly average member of the Nicholson's chain. Inside, however, it all soon changes, especially if you remember to look up at the wonderfully ornate ceiling.

Our first glance, of course, was at the bar, where we were delighted to spy Partridge beer from the Dark Star Brewing Company. It's quite sweet, almost toffee-tasting at times but in an understated way, and is a convincing attempt at producing nothing more fancy than a best bitter.

There's obviously a thing going on around here about naming pubs after railway chairmen. Just as the Lord Aberconway tips its hat to the Metropolitan railway, there's a Wetherspoon's pub on the station concourse called the Hamilton Hall. This one's named after Lord Claud Hamilton, a former chairman of the Great Eastern Railway Company. So there.

WILLIAMS ALE AND CIDER HOUSE

HOW TO GET THERE

The nearest tube station, and indeed mainline station, to The Williams (as they call themselves on their website) is Liverpool Street, which is reached by no fewer than four different underground lines: Central (the red one), Circle (yellow), Metropolitan (magenta) and Hammersmith and City (pink).

When you leave Liverpool Street underground station, you should see a pub called The Railway directly in front of you. Actually, you'll probably see a lot of roadworks, but the pub should still be visible. You'll be on the corner of Old Broad Street and Liverpool Street, and you want to turn right and walk along Liverpool Street, with the entrance to the mainline station on your left.

Carry on until you reach the junction with Bishopsgate (The George pub is on the corner), and turn left to walk down Bishopsgate. After wandering past the intriguingly named Catherine Wheel Alley and the more prosaic Middlesex Street, Artillery Lane will be on the right. It's not a very wide lane and is easily missed, so keep an eye out for a pub called The Woodin's Shades and a branch of NatWest Bank. Turn right immediately after the bank, and walk a short way down Artillery Lane until The Williams can be seen on the right.

LOCAL INFORMATION

As you will probably have gathered by now, there are a lot of pubs in this area, and Catherine Wheel Alley is named after one of them. Unfortunately, you can't visit The Catherine Wheel pub, because it was demolished in 1911.

One place you can visit is Old Spitalfields Market. If you temporarily ignore Artillery Lane and carry on along Bishopsgate and take the next right down Brushfield Street, you'll find the market on your left. Turning left on Commercial Street as it crosses Brushfield Street, you'll soon see a pub called The Ten Bells, which is worth a visit in its own right.

Astonishingly, there are records of a market having been here since 1638, thanks to King Charles granting the licence to trade. Even some of the current buildings date back as far as 1887, with various extensions over the years, most notably westward in 1926. It's fair to say that you'll find an eclectic range of goods on sale here, so we'd highly recommend a browse if you've got time to spare before visiting the pub.

22-24 Artillery Lane, London E1 7LS
Open: Mon-Wed 11am-11pm, Thu-Sat 11pm-midnight, Sun closed
Food: Mon-Sat noon-4pm
Tel: 020 7247 5163
www.williamsspitalfields.com

DESCRIPTION

The first time we walked into this pub we were struck by the marked contrast between the hustle and bustle outside, and the relative tranquillity and modest rustic charm of the interior of the pub. Having gravitated toward the bar and its selection of over a dozen ales, we opted for the interesting sounding Chockwork Orange from Brentwood Brewery Company.

We did wonder about the wisdom of starting afternoon drinks with a beer weighing in at a hefty 6.5% ABV. However, we're glad we chose it. It's a full-bodied beer, dark brown with a thin tan head, and tasting and smelling as its name implies, with subtle chocolate and orange notes definitely present. Overall, it was nicely balanced, with a sweet and slightly fruity citrus taste. It certainly put us in a good mood, as we gazed around at the old wooden floors and regarded an ancient piano that looks as if it's only where it is to keep the cellar hatchway shut and to stop people accidentally (or deliberately) falling into the cellar. However, it does get used fairly regularly.

There's quite a collection of old pub prints around the walls, a rather marvellous etched mirror with an ornate golden frame, and thankfully in this age of mobile phones and laptops, a collection of daily newspapers on offer for some quiet reading.

THE GEORGE

HOW TO GET THERE

Your nearest tube station for The George is London Bridge, which is on the Bank branch of the Northern line. Out of a number of exits you want the one that will take you to Borough Street East. If you emerge on the same side of the road as Borough Market, you'll need to cross over to the other side. However you manage to get there, you should start walking along Borough High Street away from the station exit. If you find yourself walking past Barclays Bank then you're going the wrong way: turn around and set off in the opposite direction.

Just a few yards away from the station is King's Head Yard, home to The Old King's Head pub. If you've got some time to spare then by all means give it a go, but it pales into insignificance when compared to The George.

King's Head Yard makes a reappearance in a short while as it turns around and doubles back on itself, and then The George is down the next alleyway along. Walk down the alleyway towards the pub, and prepare to step back in time.

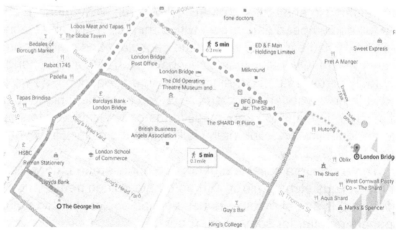

LOCAL INFORMATION

The George is in Southwark, a historic part of London, and can trace its roots back to the 10th century. It even gets a mention in The Domesday Book in 1086. In 1307 we find mention of another historic old pub in the area. This was The Tabard, which traded as an inn for over 500 years, although it was rather controversially pulled down in 1873 despite a public outcry. It was referenced in Chaucer's Canterbury Tales, which is a fine claim to fame.

John Harvard was born and went to school in Southwark, where his father ran a pub. He later moved to America and left the majority of his wealth to a new university which, in honour of the gesture, named itself after him. Harvard University was established in 1636, and to date has produced eight American Presidents.

Guy's hospital (we're up to 1721 now) is at the back of The George, and acquired a lot of land from it, leaving The George to be only about one-fifth of the size that it used to be. Before it disappears completely, and we sincerely hope that this is a long, long time away, let's get a drink.

75-77 Borough High St, London SE1 1NH
Open: Mon-Sat 11am-11pm, Sun noon-10.30pm
Food: Mon-Sat 11am-10pm, Sun noon-9pm
Tel: 020 7407 2056
www.george-southwark.co.uk

DESCRIPTION

The George is maintained by the National Trust, and the beer is provided by Greene King, which will have some people groaning, but it's a decent enough range of ales for all that, and there's always a guest on if you're not a Greene King fan.

The current pub was built in 1677, and is the last surviving galleried inn in London. The pub has had many famous patrons over the years. Dickens, inevitably, came here, and mentioned the pub in Little Dorrit. Samuel Pepys is said to have proclaimed to the people below as he paraded about up in the galleries. Is it possible that Shakespeare drank in a bar that was on the site before the current inn? The Globe Theatre was just around the corner, and Shakespeare might well have wandered in. Beer writer Pete Brown puts this theory forward in his book Shakespeare's Local, a fascinating history of The George.

If the weather's nice, take your drink outside and sit in the courtyard. Looking up you can't fail to see The Shard, and you can only marvel at the contrast between the tallest building in the United Kingdom and the only galleried inn left in London. The George is probably the quintessential London pub. It's one that everybody should visit, but preferably not all at the same time.

THE MARKET PORTER

Photo courtesy of The Market Porter

HOW TO GET THERE

The Market Porter is a one-minute walk from London Bridge underground station, as long as you emerge from the correct exit. London Bridge is on the Bank branch of the Northern line so if you find yourself trundling through Charing Cross station and on the wrong branch of the line for London Bridge, just wait until you get to either Euston if you're travelling north or Kennington if you're travelling south, and change to the Bank part of the line.

London Bridge has numerous exits, and you should aim for Borough High Street (West).This, reasonably enough, will bring you on to Borough High Street. The Shard should be easily visible behind you, as it is the tallest building in Britain at 310 meters (1017 feet) and, at the time of writing, the tallest building in the European Union. After BREXIT, of course, it won't be.

There should be a pub in front of you called The Southwark Tavern (also well worth a visit), with Stoney Street to the right hand side of it. Walk past the pub and along Stoney Street, and in a matter of moments you'll see The Market Porter on the left.

LOCAL INFORMATION

There are a number of pubs in this book that occupy the area around Borough Market, and you can have a pleasant stroll exploring The Market Porter, The Rake and The George. As well as pubs, you can't fail to escape from the shadow of The Shard, and if the weather is even half decent it's worth a trip to the top. It's a bit scary when you stand next to it at ground level and look up, knowing that you're about to step into a lift that's going to take you up there, but it's worth it.

If you prefer to be at ground level, just around the corner from The Market Porter you'll find a place called The Clink Prison Museum. To get to it you should carry on along Stoney Street until you reach a T-junction with Clink Street. Turn left and the museum's on your left.

The museum is where the original prison used to be. The prison dated from 1144, and the museum is a grisly celebration of its inmates and some of the bizarre instruments of torture that were used in over 600 years of operation. If you've got questions about crime and punishment, you'll probably find the answers here.

9 Stoney St, London SE1 9AA
Open: Mon-Fri 6am-8.30am and 11am-11pm, Sat noon-11pm, Sun noon-10.30pm
Bar food: Mon-Fri noon-3pm, Sun noon-5pm; Restaurant Mon-Thu noon-3pm, Fri-Sun noon-5pm
Tel: 020 7407 2495
www.markettaverns.co.uk/the_market_porter.html

DESCRIPTION

On the other hand, if your question is, 'A pint?', The Market Porter may well have the answer. If you're a fan of the Harry Potter films, you might recognise the place as having featured in Harry Potter and the Prisoner of Azkaban, as the pub was turned into The Third Hand Book Emporium, just next to The Leaky Cauldron.

This traditional, down-to-earth pub has plenty of beer choice, no doubt about that. There can be up to ten real ales on handpump on any particular day, and a number of ciders too. On our most recent visit we had a Chocolate Orange Stout from Front Row Brewing, who are based in Cheshire. It lived up to its name, being quite sweet but with a healthy stout toastiness about it to back it all up.

The pub can get astonishingly busy at times, being across the road from Borough Market, and the customer overspill frequently heads out on to the street. There's a small seating area at the back, and an upstairs restaurant if you're trying to escape from the hordes.

THE RAKE

HOW TO GET THERE

This can be a tricky one to find when you first visit the area, even though it's only a five-minute walk from the tube station. That station is London Bridge, which is on the Bank section of the Northern line.

When leaving London Bridge station head for the exit that's on Tooley Street, leading towards London Bridge and its captivating views along the River Thames. To get to The Rake, however, you need to ignore the lure of the Thames. Turn left on leaving the tube station to walk along Tooley Street in the direction of a pub called The Barrow Boy and Banker (worth a diversion if you've got time to spare), and then turn left to walk underneath a railway bridge.

You'll find some opportunities to cross the road here, thanks to various traffic lights. Having crossed over, carry on beneath the bridge until you see a road on your right called Bedale Street. Follow that road as it heads back under the railway bridge and becomes Cathedral Street, with Southwark Cathedral to the right, and then on your left you'll see Winchester Walk. Stroll down here, and the pub is almost at the end of the street on your left.

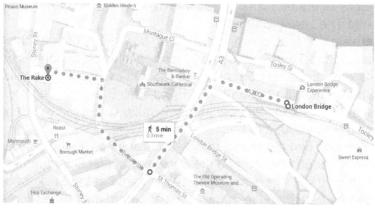

LOCAL INFORMATION

During the second part of the walk from the station to The Rake, you can't fail to notice Borough Market. This large, sprawling market celebrated its very own millennium in 2014, and its website gives an entertaining account of how its history can be traced all the way back to 1014. Then, as now, it stood near the southern end of London Bridge. At the time, the Bridge was the only walkable route across the Thames in London. Now, of course, there are dozens of them.

If you're intending to pay it a visit, the market is open in all its glory from Wednesday to Saturday, with a smaller version operating on Monday and Tuesday. It is closed on Sundays.

Many of the stalls in the market are devoted to food, but thankfully for us there is one that operates as an off-licence. Already established in Borough Market at the time, Utobeer looked to expand its business and, in 2006, converted an old cafe on the edge of the market into a bar. That bar is called The Rake, and that's where we're heading now.

14 Winchester Walk, London SE1 9AG
Open: Mon-Fri noon-11pm, Sat 11am-11pm, Sun noon-10pm
Food: Bar snacks
Tel: 020 7407 0557
www.utobeer.co.uk/the-rake

DESCRIPTION

The Rake is a bit of a grandfather on the London craft beer scene, even though it opened as recently as 2006. It's a relatively small bar, with only a limited number of cask ales on offer along with a larger number of keg lines, and the fridges behind the bar hold a big selection of bottled beers from both local breweries and ones much further afield.

The interior of the pub is functional, with a number of round wooden tables having bar stools dotted around them. It often gets packed, and you can always escape to the outdoor drinking and smoking area to the left of the front door.

On the white walls inside the bar, you'll see numerous signatures of brewers from all over the world who've visited the pub and left their mark. You'll probably recognise a lot of them, but if you're like us there'll be many that you've never heard of. Wonder if they've got any of their bottles in the fridges? Only one way to find out...

YE OLDE WATLING

HOW TO GET THERE

The closest station here is Mansion House on the Circle and District lines, although Bank (Northern and Central) and St. Paul's (Central) stations are also nearby if either of those suits you better. Mansion House has numerous exits, and you'll need Exit 1B. Make your way up to ground level to emerge on Garlick Hill, which got its name because there was a nearby wharf where shipments of garlic were landed.

Turn left on leaving the exit, and cross over the junction of Queen Victoria Street and Cannon Street, using the traffic lights just to the right of Garlick Hill. On the other side of the road you'll need to go and stand opposite Garlick Hill, because Bow Lane continues the journey on the other side of the junction. Ye Olde Watling is a short way along, on the right.

A longer walk, but with a better view, is to continue walking along Queen Victoria Street after you've crossed over, leaving Bow Lane behind you. You'll soon come to Watling Street on the left, a single-width lane with a statue in honour of shoe-makers of olden times. Continue up Watling Street and St Paul's Cathedral appears in stately fashion in the distance. St. Paul's Cathedral is very important to the history of this pub.

LOCAL INFORMATION

Watling Street has a significant role to play in the history of London, being an old Roman road that ran the breadth of the country from Dover via London and on into Wales. Thus London became an important staging post along the way.

The pub was built by Sir Christopher Wren in 1668. Like most of the surrounding areas, Watling Street was recovering after the Great Fire of London, and work was taking place throughout London as it struggled to recover from the devastation.

After the pub had been constructed, Sir Christopher Wren used an upstairs office as his drawing room while working on the construction of St Paul's Cathedral. Something to think about if you're having a meal upstairs! It is believed that some of his workmen stayed in the place while working on the same project.

It's only a short walk to St. Pauls, and it's such a beautiful Baroque building that you're almost honour-bound to go and see it. If you're feeling particularly athletic, you can climb the 528 steps inside the cathedral to reach the Golden Gallery and look out at some great views of London.

29 Watling St, London EC4M 9BR
Open: Mon-Fri 10am-11pm, Sat noon-8pm, Sun noon-5pm
Tel: 020 7248 8935
www.nicholsonspubs.co.uk/restaurants/london/
yeoldewatlingwatlingstreetlondon

DESCRIPTION

Try to avoid coming here early evening, especially later in the week, as it gets very busy indeed. We usually try to arrive mid-afternoon when it's re-covering from the mid-day trade and bracing itself for the early evening rush.

Inside you'll find a pub that has been tastefully restored, with plenty of wood panelling, and a decorative bar with an imposing array of cask and keg ales on offer. One time when we went in, they had a milk stout on, and the landlord confessed that he'd never tried one before. Well, it was a decent stout, and it had an understated lactose-induced milk taste to it, so we hope he liked it.

Sir Christopher Wren is honoured, as you would expect being so close to the cathedral, and there are pleasing numbers of prints on the wall depicting some of his works.

Our notes on a recent visit finished with: 'Why can't all Nicholson's pubs be like this? We don't all like, or want, overloud thumpy thumpy back-ground music'. We'd obviously had enough beer by then to send us firmly into the grumpy old men stage. Happily, Ye Olde Watling bucks the trend of many pubs and manages to function perfectly nicely as just that: a pub.

THE THREE TUNS

HOW TO GET THERE

The closest tube station to the Three Tuns is Marble Arch, which is on the Central (red) line, and thus connects up nicely with the likes of Shepherd's Bush and Notting Hill Gate to the west, along with places such as Oxford Circus, Tottenham Court Road and Holborn to the east.

Getting from Marble Arch station to the Three Tuns is quite straightforward, although there are numerous exits waiting to fool you and send you off in completely the wrong direction. You want to go for Exit 1, which will place you on the north side of Oxford Street.

When you come out of the station, turn left to walk along Oxford Street, resisting the lure of the shops until you reach Portman Street on your left. Cross over it at the traffic lights, and then turn left to walk up the far side of Portman Street. The second turning on your right will be Portman Mews South, just after Granville Place, and walking into Portman Mews South will soon see the Three Tuns appearing on your right hand side.

LOCAL INFORMATION

Marble Arch, the white marble arch from which the station takes its name, was designed in 1827, and thus predates the underground station by 73 years. It was 1833 before the Arch was completed for the first time, but it hasn't always stood where it is now.

When it was first built, it stood as the entrance to the then new Buckingham Palace, but when expansion work on the Palace was started in 1847, the Arch was dismantled and taken piece by piece to the north east corner of Hyde Park, where it was put back together again to form a grand entrance into the Park.

All was well until the early 1960s when road 'improvements' meant that Marble Arch became pretty much isolated on a small island, where it looks lost and a little vulnerable as traffic roars past almost immediately in front of it. Nonetheless, it remains an enduring image of London, and will have been the subject of millions of photographs by millions of tourists. Go on, you know you want to.

1 Portman Mews South, London W1H 6HR
Open: Daily 11am-11pm
Food: Mon-Sat 11am-11pm, Sun 11am-10.30pm
Tel: 020 7408 0330
www.taylor-walker.co.uk/pub/three-tuns-marylebone/c0728

DESCRIPTION

If you thought that The Three Tuns looks like two separate buildings, you'd be right. One goes back to 1764, and later they took over the building next door, with the current frontage of the pub dating from 1871. Being two separate buildings originally, it would be too much of a coincidence to think that they were both built on the same level inside, and there is a small difference in height to be negotiated when walking from one part of the pub to the other.

The pub is run by Taylor Walker, but why is it Three Tuns, not Three Tons? A ton is a unit of weight, whereas a tun is a large barrel containing 216 gallons of beer, hence the three images incorporated inside the signage displaying the name of the pub over the door.

There's usually a good atmosphere in this comfortable old pub, whichever part of it you're sitting in, and it's good to see that a recent refurbishment has been sensitive to this very British of buildings with its collection of nooks and crannies. The beer range isn't spectacular, but they do look after it well (whenever we've been in it has tasted on good form), and their food is traditional and, for this part of London so close to Oxford Street, reasonably priced.

THE SIR JOHN BALCOMBE

Photo courtesy of The Sir John Balcombe

HOW TO GET THERE

Marylebone Underground Station is your nearest port of call for this one, with Paddington about a mile to the west and Euston around a mile to the east. It's on the Bakerloo line, which gives you direct access from the likes of Charing Cross, Piccadilly Circus, Oxford Circus and Baker Street.

When you walk out of the front of the station, take a sharp left onto Melcombe Place. Your first left turn will be Boston Place, but ignore that and keep on walking down the road for a little while until you reach Balcombe Street. At this point turn left, and the pub will soon appear on the right-hand side of the road.

LOCAL INFORMATION

There are attractions galore in this part of London. If you're a fan of the works of Sir Arthur Conan Doyle, you might want to carry on walking along Melcombe Place until you see Baker Street in front of you. There, you should turn left, and at – of course – 221b Baker Street, you'll find the Sherlock Holmes Museum. It opens at 9.30 every day and closes at 6pm, so a lunchtime visit is recommended. It's also just along the road from The Beatles Store, a huge collection of all things fab.

If you follow Baker Street a little bit further on from the Sherlock Holmes Museum you'll come to Regent's Park, which will reward an exploration. It's the home of what is popularly known as London Zoo, and also houses Queen Mary's Gardens, where you'll find over 400 different varieties of roses.

21 Balcombe St, London NW1 6HE
Open: Mon-Sat 11am-11pm, Sun 11am-10.30pm
Food: Mon-Fri noon-10pm, Sat-Sun noon-9pm
Tel: 020 3601 0167
www.sjohnbalcombenw1.co.uk

DESCRIPTION

The Sir John Balcombe is owned and operated by the Bermondsey Beer Company (part of the vast Enterprise chain), which maintains quite a varied portfolio of pubs. The real Sir John Balcombe was a QC who practised at the Chancery Bar (not a pub!). He later became a judge (1977) and was knighted in the same year. The pub re-opened towards the end of 2014, and has a nice woody theme throughout, with an interesting collection of various items scattered around its interior. Fans of clocks will feel at home.

It's not the sort of place you'd describe as a traditional London boozer. There's a 'craft' feel to it all, but it's friendly and welcoming, and the food is good old British pub grub. There's also a cellar bar available for hire, complete with piano, and the walls are adorned with several framed newspapers that describe the siege of Balcombe Street in 1975 when four members of the IRA were holed up in a flat at 22b Balcombe Street for six days until the police successfully negotiated a surrender.

There were four beers on when we visited last, and although we've seen a few negative reviews on TripAdvisor, we have to go with the majority and say that the beer was spot on. Our pints of Timothy Taylor's Landlord, a beer notoriously difficult to keep in top form, were marvellous.

THE CROSSE KEYS

Photo courtesy of The Crosse Keys

HOW TO GET THERE

You're aiming for Monument tube station for this one, and you can get there on either the Circle (yellow) or the District (green) lines. There are several exits from Monument, which can get confusing, and we always aim for the Fish Street Hill one. It's not the most obvious one for getting to the Crosse Keys, but at least we know where we are when we step into the outside world. Sir Christopher Wren's Monument to the Great Fire of London is off to the right, and it's always worth taking a moment to gaze at it. Of the 80,000 or so people living in the city of London at the time of the Great Fire in 1666, almost 90% of them lost their homes.

Turn left out of the tube station and walk up Fish Street Hill until you reach Eastcheap Road. Crossing here will take you to Gracechurch Street, and if you follow the pedestrian crossings you should end up on the left hand side of Gracechurch Street. If you arrive on the right hand side, you'll need to cross over somewhere. Keep walking up Gracechurch Street and it won't be long before The Crosse Keys appears on your left. You can't miss it. It's enormous.

LOCAL INFORMATION

Wetherspoon pubs tend to be seen as a rather new 21st-century concept, and the individual pubs nowadays go under the banner nickname of 'Spoons', but the first one was opened in Muswell Hill in 1979. You can't go and pay tribute to it, because the oldest surviving Spoons dates back to 1983. Based in Stoke Newington, it is called the Rochester Castle.

Wetherspoon was founded by Tim Martin, and he has stated that the name 'Wetherspoon' comes from a geography teacher of his when he was a young child being educated at a primary school in New Zealand.

They are generally large pubs, and for all that people sometimes rail against them, they are often sympathetic conversions of premises that were never intended to be pubs. Old banks, cinemas, post offices, churches (the Richard Oastler in Brighouse, West Yorkshire, is a splendid example of a church that is now a pub), all feature in the Wetherspoon collection.

The names of the pubs quite often reflect local culture. For example, The Crosse Keys is named after an old coaching inn that used to stand close by the site of the present pub.

9 Gracechurch St, London EC3V 0DR
Open: Mon-Thu 8am-11pm, Fri 8am-midnight, Sat 9am-11pm, Sun 9.30am-6.30pm
Tel: 020 7623 4824
https://www.jdwetherspoon.com/pubs/all-pubs/england/london/the-crosse-keys-city-of-london

DESCRIPTION

The Crosse Keys is immense, a vast giant of a pub with marble columns, elegant ceilings, a huge oval bar, and over 20 beers to choose from. On a recent visit, there were eight people working behind the bar, who were only serving beer. Add on the number of staff involved on the catering side, and you're approaching something the size of a small village.

Happily, there are monitors above the bar that cycle through the available beers, and when you spot one that you would like to drink, go and stand near a till and ask for a pint of whatever number you've decided to drink. Don't ask for a name of a beer, just ask for a number. Standing near a till seems to give faster service, although we couldn't fault the speed of service on any of our visits.

Like any central London pub it can get rather packed, and even somewhere as big as the Crosse Keys can be crowded at times. However, there are enough tables (and an escape upstairs to a balcony at the back of the pub) to find somewhere to sit and contemplate the rather lengthy lunch hours that some London city workers seem to enjoy.

THE LAMB TAVERN

HOW TO GET THERE

We're getting two pubs for the price of one here, because The Lamb Tavern stands brick to brick beside Old Tom's Bar. But first you'll need to get to Monument station, which is served by the Circle and District lines.

We usually head for the Fish Street Hill exit, which has an advantage and a disadvantage. The advantage is that it lets you take a close look at Sir Christopher Wren's famous monument to the Great Fire of London, from which the station takes its name. You can climb the 311 steps to the top of the Monument if you're feeling energetic, but the rest of us are going to the pub.

The disadvantage is that when you get back to the station from the Monument and keep on heading north, you'll soon have to cross Eastcheap Road to allow you to proceed up Gracechurch Street. Keep on along Gracechurch Street, and soon after you pass a large pub called The Crosse Keys on your left, the entrance to Leadenhall Market will appear on the right. Just walk into the enclosed market, and the fabulous exterior surrounding The Lamb Tavern will very soon come into view.

LOCAL INFORMATION

There has been a market on the site of Leadenhall Market since the 14th century, although the present interior is much younger. The incredibly ornate roof and cobbled floor were designed in 1881, and take time to study the roof before plunging into the pub. This isn't a Grade II listed building for nothing.

When you walk in, you may think that you've seen this building somewhere before. If you're a fan of Harry Potter you'll recognise it from the film Harry Potter and the Philosopher's Stone, where an optician's in Bull's Head Passage was used as the entrance to The Leaky Cauldron. Some of the exterior Diagon Alley scenes were also filmed here.

Old Tom's Bar next door to The Lamb Tavern takes its name from a character who used to live in the market in the early 1800s, but this character wasn't a man or a woman. It was a gander. Like countless other ganders it was destined to be slaughtered, but managed to escape. He was known to everyone in the market, and all the inns used to feed him. He acquired the nickname Old Tom and lived to the grand old age of 37. He's buried in the market.

10-12 Leadenhall Market, London EC3V 1LR
Open: Mon-Fri 11am-11pm
Food: Mon-Fri noon-9pm
Tel: 020 7626 2454
www.lambtavernleadenhall.com

DESCRIPTION

The Lamb Tavern was first built in 1309, although a sign in the current building states that it was established in 1780. As befits such a venerable history, it is an architectural gem. It's also a Young's brewery house, and five of its beers were available on one visit, including the seasonal Winter Warmer. Its current strength of 5.0% is just about right for a refreshing lunchtime drink, especially if you climbed to the top of the Monument before coming here.

We supped our drinks beneath a picture of a smiling Queen Mother pouring a pint of Young's Special. Above her is a picture of Prince Charles attempting the same feat, although with a good deal less confidence than his grandmother. On a later jaunt we noticed that the Queen Mum had been moved upstairs, although Prince Charles remained in his place.

The pub can get very busy at lunchtimes and in the early evening, so it's best to arrive either very early or in the middle of the afternoon. When we popped in recently, there were three customers in the pub at 12 o'clock, and by half-past it was packed.

THE SHIP

Photo courtesy of The Ship

HOW TO GET THERE

The nearest station for The Ship is Monument, on the Circle (yellow) and District (green) lines. The Circle line is handy for many places, but for tube trivia fans it no longer does a complete circle. It did when it opened in 1884 but the circle was broken in 2009 and now you are forced to change at Edgware Road.

The District line can be confusing at first as it splits into several different branches in its western sections, but from Gloucester Road heading east you've only got the one branch. As long as it says Tower Hill, Barking or Upminster on the front of the tube train, you're safe.

There are several exits at Monument, and the one that we normally take is the Fish Street Hill exit. It might not be the nearest or most convenient, but we know where we are when we leave the station. Turn left and walk up to Eastcheap, cross over at the traffic lights, and carry on onto Gracechurch Street. Keep going in the same direction and watch for a narrow roadway on your right called Talbot Court. At the time of writing, it's just past a branch of Santander bank. Turn into the Court, and you'll soon see The Ship in front of you.

LOCAL INFORMATION

Sir Christopher Wren's Monument commemorates the Great Fire of London in 1666. However, it is not at the spot where the fire first broke out, and historians have recently told us that it started approximately 202 feet away, in what is now called Monument Street.

In 1666, however, the current Monument Street would have been designated as Pudding Lane, and it wasn't until the late 19th century that Monument Street came into being as various properties nearby were demolished to make way for it. One such property was the building that used to be a bakery belonging to Thomas Fariner. Sparks from his oven struck some fuel and started the blaze that would be responsible for the destruction of 80% of London's property over the next five days.

To get to the spot where the fire is believed to have started, turn right on leaving Monument underground station from the Fish Street Hill exit. Head towards the Monument itself, then turn immediately left after it. This will shortly bring you to the junction with Pudding Lane, but cross over and take three or four more steps further forwards and you'll be on Monument Street and the place where the horror all began.

11 Talbot Court, London EC3V 0BP
Open: Mon-Fri 11am-11pm, Sat 11am-6pm, Sun closed
Tel: 020 7929 3903
www.nicholsonspubs.co.uk/restaurants/london/theshiptalbotcourtlondon

DESCRIPTION

The Ship is part of the Nicholson's chain of pubs, which means that you can expect an old traditional building and a decent range of beers. Imagine lots of dark wood, a curved wooden bar, plenty of ale and an escape route upstairs to a normally quieter dining area.

The pub stands on the same site as an old coaching inn called The Talbot, which was destroyed during the Great Fire of 1666. A Talbot was a now-extinct hunting dog, believed to be a forerunner of the present-day Beagle, and plenty of people claim that it was brought to Britain by William the Conqueror in the 11th century. It's a nice story, without a shred of evidence to support it.

When the pub was rebuilt it was called The Ship due to the large number of people who frequented the bar and worked in local ports on the Thames. These days it's more likely to be full of loud-mouthed suit-wearing people from nearby offices, but don't let them put you off. On our last visit we had a pint of Wainwright, formerly from Thwaites' brewery but now brewed by Marston's. At heart this is a quaint, old-fashioned boozer, and there's nothing wrong with that.

THE WALRUS AND THE CARPENTER

HOW TO GET THERE

If you're travelling here by tube, you'll be arriving at Monument Station by either the Circle (yellow) or District (green) lines. If you're on the District line, anywhere heading east from Earl's Court will do, so if you're at any of Sloane Square, Victoria, Westminster or Embankment stops, step on to the first train that's heading towards Tower Hill, Barking, or Upminster, and you'll soon be there.

As with every other Monument pub in this book, and there are quite a few, we'd leave the underground station via the Fish Street Hill exit. Pages elsewhere will direct you to The Lamb Tavern, Uncle Tom's Bar, The Crosse Keys and The Ship, but this one's taking us to The Walrus and The Carpenter.

Turn right on leaving via the Fish Street Hill exit, and then turn left on to Monument Street just after passing by the Monument itself. Keep going along Monument Street, and as you go you'll pass by the spot where the Great Fire of London started in 1666 (just across the junction with Pudding Lane). When the road starts to bend around to the right towards Lower Thames Street, you'll see the pub in front of you on your left hand side.

LOCAL INFORMATION
The pub's named after the poem, as spoken by Tweedledee and Tweedledum in Lewis Carroll's book Through The Looking-Glass. The writer's real name was Charles Lutwidge Dodgson, although to this day he is still better known as Lewis Carroll. It's a wonderfully bizarre piece of writing, and here's an extract:

> 'The time has come,' the Walrus said,
> 'To talk of many things:
> Of shoes—and ships—and sealing-wax—
> Of cabbages—and kings—
> and why the sea is boiling hot—
> and whether pigs have wings.'

He was also a gifted photographer, as well as being a mathematical lecturer at Christ Church in Oxford. He invented numerous popular games, such as the Word Ladder, which consisted of taking a word and, by changing it one letter at a time, would end up with a completely different word. For example, start with HIVE, alter V to R for HIRE, change the H to get WIRE, swap the I to get WORE, and finally amend the letter E to get WORK. There was no Internet in Victorian times!

45 Monument St, London EC3R 8BU
Open: Mon-Fri 11am-11pm, Sat noon-8pm, Sun closed
Tel: 020 7621 1647
www.nicholsonspubs.co.uk/restaurants/london/
thewalrusandthecarpentermonumentlondon

DESCRIPTION
The best time to arrive here is around mid-afternoon, because lunchtimes and early evenings get very busy with people in suits who allegedly work in the nearby financial areas of the city. The Walrus and The Carpenter is part of the Nicholson's chain, but has a more extensive range of beers for sale than a lot of them, and there were ten different cask ales on offer when we were last there. We were surprised to see Rudgate Brewery's Ruby Mild here (it's a long way from Yorkshire), but we bought a couple of pints anyway, and this smooth, slightly smoky, mild went down a treat. Top marks to whoever looks after the cellar.

You've got the Lewis Carroll dining room upstairs in addition to the downstairs bar, but on a recent visit we were standing outside having a drink and overheard the most wonderful quote, the sort of thing that you really can't make up. It was about eight o'clock at night, and a couple in their late twenties were embracing before parting for the evening. Both were smartly dressed, and after they stepped away from the embrace, friendly rather than romantic, she looked at him and said, 'Oh, I just can't wait to get home and hug my donkey.' Fair enough.

KEATS AT THE GLOBE

HOW TO GET THERE

The Globe is a straightforward pub to find, as long as you exit from Moorgate underground station onto Moorgate and not Moorfields. Metropolitan, Circle, Northern, and Hammersmith and City lines all pass through here, giving easy access from numerous popular spots in the city. If you're on the Northern line, just make sure that you're on the Bank section of it rather than the Charing Cross one.

When you leave your train and head towards the way out, look for the exit for Finsbury Square, which will place you on the west side of Moorgate. A few steps to the right you'll see a street named Moor Place, but ignore that and keep walking along Moorgate.

Within a minute or so of leaving the tube station and going along Moorgate, you'll see the pub appear on your right hand side. At first glance it looks as if there could be two pubs here, one called The Globe and another named Keats at the Globe, and years ago they were indeed two separate establishments, but now it's all part of the same pub under the Nicholson's banner.

LOCAL INFORMATION

So... why is one part of the pub called The Globe and the other part called Keats at the Globe? The Globe is the original pub, whereas Keats at the Globe used to be a different pub entirely. It's had a number of names over the years (The Swan and Hoop, The Moorgate), and although it can't be claimed with 100% accuracy that the English poet John Keats was born on the premises, we do know that his father managed the stables that used to be at the inn. Nowadays, it is just a separate room from the main bar area of The Globe.

If by some happy chance you are here on 31st October, you can raise a glass in his honour and celebrate John Keats' birthday, because baptismal records show that he was born on the 31st October, 1795. Strange that one of the great Romantic Poets should be born on Halloween. Keats always claimed that he'd been born at the inn, but there isn't any firm evidence for it.

Keats's most famous works are found in the series of Odes that he composed, such as Ode on a Grecian Urn, or Ode to a Nightingale.

We're about to have our own ode: Ode to a Pint.

83 Moorgate, London EC2M 6SA
Open: Mon-Fri 10am-11.30pm, Sat noon-5pm, Sun closed
Tel: 020 7374 2915
www.nicholsonspubs.co.uk/restaurants/london/theglobemoorgatelondon

DESCRIPTION

Our notes refer to The Globe as a fine old Victorian pub, with eight cask ales on sale. Being a Nicholson's establishment, you can be reasonably assured of a fair collection of different beers. According to Nicholson's website, the globe is an historic emblem of Portugal, and centuries ago it was used to advertise pubs selling fine Portuguese wines.

We couldn't see much evidence of Portuguese wines when we were last there, but that may be because we weren't looking. We'd found a pump clip bearing Scottish brewery William Brothers' Fraoch, a lovely amber ale whose recipe is said to date back to 2000 BC. It's quite spicy, brewed using heather, and is marvellously peaty with that spicy flavour going on with every mouthful. Beer that's brewed to a 4000 year old recipe? Works for us, and we hope you find it there in this wonderful old pub, which always has plenty of excellent beers to choose from.

THE CHURCHILL ARMS

HOW TO GET THERE

The nearest underground station to The Churchill Arms is Notting Hill Gate, which is on the Central, District and Circle lines. Thus it is within easy reach of Oxford Circus (Central), Earl's Court (District), Victoria (Circle), and many other popular destinations. As you come through the ticket barriers at the station, turn left and then left again to go up the steps onto Notting Hill Gate. Walk ahead and turn right at the lights onto Kensington Church Street.

From there it's a brief stroll to The Churchill Arms. It's easy enough to recognise the pub because of the mass of flowers hanging outside it. This makes it one of the most photogenic pubs in London.

If you arrive on a Saturday, almost as soon as you turn on to Kensington Church Street you'll find yourself beside Notting Hill Farmers Market. This is as good a chance as any to stock up on some extremely fresh fruit and vegetables. If you're only here for the beer, ignore the market and carry on towards the pub.

LOCAL INFORMATION

Notting Hill is, of course, home to the popular Notting Hill Carnival. This usually takes place on the last weekend in August, taking in the August Bank Holiday. Notting Hill gets extremely busy during this time, so The Churchill Arms is perhaps best left alone if you're only making a casual visit. On the other hand, if the Carnival is your thing, party on.

119 Kensington Church St, London W8 7LN
Open: Mon-Wed 11am-11pm, Thu-Sat 11am-midnight, Sun noon-10.30pm
Food: Mon-Sat noon-10pm, Sun noon-9.30pm
Tel: 020 7727 4242
www.churchillarmskensington.co.uk

DESCRIPTION

The pub was built in 1750, and has seen many famous visitors over the years. Among them were Winston Churchill's grandparents, who drank here in the 1800s, and from whom the pub takes its name. Today it is an old-fashioned boozer packed with Churchill memorabilia.

They take the theme to heart, and sometimes have party nights focussing on the 1940s. It is a strange feeling indeed to walk in of an evening and find the place packed full of people dressed as if they were celebrating the end of the Second World War, while you stand there in your modern clothes wondering if you've stepped through a time warp.

Another time when we went, we ended up sitting at a table next to a plaque on the wall bearing some of Churchill's most memorable quotes. It was inspiring to read the familiar lines, especially: 'We shall fight them on the beaches ... we shall never surrender'.

If you're in London in the couple of weeks before Christmas, that's the perfect time to pay an evening visit here. Down come the floral decorations and up go the Christmas lights, seemingly bigger and better every year. Landlord Gerry O'Brien has been doing it for about thirty years now, and uses upwards of 20,000 lights and 90 trees. It's truly a sight to behold.

The pub is owned by Fuller's Brewery, so you know what sort of beers to expect. Appropriately, given the theme, London Pride is usually one of them. The beer takes its name from the nickname given to a small flower that started to grow on bomb sites during the blitz of London in the 1940s. This was the first London pub to serve Thai Food. It must also be one of the only pubs to win an award at the Chelsea Flower Show!

THE OLD COFFEE HOUSE

HOW TO GET THERE

If you're visiting this pub for the first time, it can be a little bit tricky to track down at night. During daylight hours, however, it's relatively straightforward. The nearest tube station is Piccadilly Circus on the Piccadilly line. Oxford Circus (Bakerloo, Central and Victoria lines) is a few minutes further away but the pub is easier to find from there.

Leave Oxford Circus by Exit 2 and walk straight ahead, so that you're going south down Regent Street. When you see Beak Street on your left (it's the one after Tenison Court), turn into Beak Street and the pub is on the left-hand side at the junction with Marshall Street. This is the street after Carnaby Street, which you might have heard of.

LOCAL INFORMATION

Tube trivia: Oxford Circus is the busiest tube station on the network. Recent figures show that almost 100 million people use Oxford Circus station during the course of a year, so it's a good idea to avoid the rush hour. Piccadilly Circus has about half that number, but it can still get extremely busy.

Oxford Circus has lots of shops and, well, that's about it. If you want to explore before going to the pub, then ignore the Beak Street turning and walk down to Piccadilly Circus, which is a great place to see. The sheer volume of people and traffic can be overwhelming at first, and in the evening the vast number of overhead flashing neon signs has become a tourist attraction in its own right. You also have to look at the Shaftesbury Memorial Fountain (we're just around the corner from Shaftesbury Avenue and its collection of theatres, bars, restaurants, nightclubs, and just about anything else you can think of). The winged sculpture at the top of the fountain is commonly referred to as Eros, although it is actually meant to represent his equally mythical brother Anteros. Whoever he is, he's become one of London's most iconic images.

49 Beak Street, London W1F 9SF
Open: Mon-Sat 11am-11pm, Sun noon-10.30pm
Tel: 020 7437 2197
Website: None

DESCRIPTION

The pub is owned by Brodie's Beers, who set up in 2008 in the east end of London. Their brewery tap, The King William IV, is a marvellous place to drink their beer, but falls outside this book's rule that every pub must be within a 10-minute walk of a tube station. However, The Old Coffee House is an excellent substitute.

This 18th-century boozer comes complete with an extensive display of vintage mirrors from breweries, alongside various beer-related signs and pictures. You can also expect a number of Brodie's own beers to be on offer. On our most recent visit we had a pint of Jamaica Stout, which was pretty smoky and had plenty of coffee and chocolate flavours. It comes in a variety of different recipes, including chilli and ginger, so you never know what might be on when you visit.

There is also a small but interesting collection of memorabilia associated with former England footballer David Beckham, including a fascinating letter written by the young David to the man who used to be his football coach. We don't know whether Victoria Beckham has read the letter, but if she has then we'd imagine that some of the content would make her blush. You'll have to visit the pub and find the letter to know what we're talking about.

THE MAD BISHOP AND BEAR

Photo courtesy of The Mad Bishop and Bear

HOW TO GET THERE

Paddington station is served by a number of different lines, as befits a station that was on the world's first underground line. The Bakerloo, Circle, District, and Hammersmith and City lines all run through here.

The pub is a simple enough one to find, because it's located on Paddington train station. To get there from Paddington underground station, there are a number of routes. For the most reliable one, locate the exit pointing you towards Ladbroke Grove. Emerge into daylight and turn right on to Praed Street. Cross over to the other side of the road when you can, taking care because the traffic is usually pretty busy around here, and take a left along London Street.

Paddington Station will now be in front of you. Enter the station at any convenient point, walk past the shopping area (Boots, Sainsburys, Marks and Spencer, the usual suspects), and when you reach Yo Sushi restaurant you'll see an escalator on the right. Take the short journey to the top, and the pub will be in front of you. You'll probably see the signs advertising the pub before you get to it.

LOCAL INFORMATION

No visitor to Paddington should overlook the opportunity to visit the Paddington Bear shop. Indeed, it is Paddington that gives the pub the 'and Bear' bit of its name. We'll get to the Mad Bishop later. The shop is, of course, dedicated to the great bear himself. Among other attractions on the station, if you arrive between Easter and Christmas at about 7.30 on a Friday night, you'll see and hear the Great Western Railway Band playing on one of the platforms. Stirring stuff.

There's also another good bar on the station concourse, next to platform 11, and this is called The Beer House. There's a good selection of beers from around the world, and how can you not like a bar whose website features this quote from Humphrey Bogart: 'The problem with the world is that everyone is a few drinks behind'. They're at: http://thebeerhouseuk.com/locations/paddington

First Floor, Paddington Station, London W2 1HB
Open: Mon-Sat 8am-11pm, Sun 10am-10.30pm
Food: Mon-Sat 8am-9.30pm, Sun 10am-9.30pm
Tel: 020 7402 2441
www.madbishopandbear.co.uk

DESCRIPTION

Ah yes, the Mad Bishop. Back in Saxon times, all the land that is now occupied by Paddington Station had been given to the Church by King Edgar. In the 1830s, the Great Western Railway was expanding rapidly and needed the land to build their new station. The Church agreed to sell the land for a very small fee, and the bishop who approved the sale was deemed to be mad because of the price.

The pub itself is rather nice, with plenty of wood dotted about the place, a marble floor, a number of mirrors, a splendid chandelier and a couple of handy monitors showing you the train departure times. A 20-minute delay no longer provokes howls of dismay, these are transformed into: 'Oh good, time for another pint'. That pint may well be a Fuller's one, as it is they who run the pub. However, unlike some Fuller's pubs, you'll get quite a number of guest beers here as well. People like Adnams, Castle Rock (the splendid Harvest Pale), St Austell and others are all likely to be spotted here.

And, of course, there is great joy to be had in taking your pint outside to the front of the pub and watching commuters scurrying by while you relax, sit back, and enjoy your drink. If you go on their website and sign up to their mailing list, they'll even give you a free pint of Fuller's finest! What more could you want?

THE WHITE HORSE

HOW TO GET THERE

The closest tube station to The White Horse is Parsons Green, and this is only served by the District line. You'll need to make sure that you're on the Wimbledon branch of the line, but if the overhead monitors aren't advertising a Wimbledon service then catch the first one that turns up and change at Earl's Court.

The pub's not too difficult to find, as long as you walk out through the correct exit, otherwise it will all go horribly wrong. As soon as you see a sign saying Parsons Green Lane, point yourself in that direction, and turn right after leaving the tube station and walk along Parsons Green Lane.

The pub will be on the left after a couple of minutes, where Parsons Green Lane connects with Ackmar Road, which means that you'll have to cross over the road at some point. There are no traffic lights and no zebra crossings between the tube station and the pub; you'll have to seize the moment.

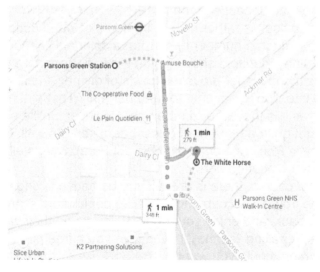

LOCAL INFORMATION
It's hard to believe it now, but this tube station first opened in March 1880. At the time, Rutherford B. Hayes was President of America, having succeeded Ulysses. S. Grant some three years earlier. Emperor Meiji was Emperor of Japan, Queen Victoria sat on the throne in England, and Benjamin Disraeli was Prime Minister of England, although he was soon to give way to William Ewart Gladstone.

If you carry on walking past the pub you will go by the side of Parsons Green itself, a grassy area allegedly named after a former vicar of Fulham. It's a pleasant enough place to stroll around, and if you plan ahead and come here on a Sunday, turn right at the end of the Green and walk down New King's Road until you reach Parsons Green Farmers' Market. It will only take you a couple of minutes, and you'll soon be filling up your shopping baskets with all manner of interesting produce. But we're here for the pub, so let's go to it.

1-3 Parsons Green, London SW6 4UL
Open: Sun-Wed 9.30am-11.30pm, Thu-Sat 9.30am-midnight
Tel: 020 7736 2115
www.whitehorsesw6.com

DESCRIPTION
This fine Victorian building boasts an extensive wooden panelled bar, with a wide range of ales from all over the world. There's over a dozen different beers to sample on cask and keg, and over 100 bottled beers to choose from, so you should find something that takes your fancy.

You might enjoy your drink while sitting on one of the long green padded benches that nestle behind lengthy wooden tables, or you might decide to stroll around the wooden floor for a while before perching beside one of the numerous tables that are dotted about the place. There are a number of separate dining areas as well, including two upstairs rooms that are available for private hire, but as always, this comes with the reminder to book in advance if you're planning a meal here.

They obviously take their beer seriously here, as they have a number of different beer festivals throughout the year. There was an American Beer Festival being promoted when we were last in, with an Old Ale Festival coming up later on in the year (we'll be back for that!) There are also various tap takeovers throughout the year, when one brewery gets to dominate the bar. Overall, The White Horse is a nice mixture of old and new, resulting in a pub that should appeal to a wide spectrum of people. It certainly appealed to us.

CASK PUB & KITCHEN

HOW TO GET THERE

CASK Pub & Kitchen is in Pimlico, and as you might expect, the nearest tube station is indeed Pimlico. It's only on the Victoria line and doesn't interchange with any other lines, although that does make it convenient for the likes of Victoria, Euston, King's Cross and Oxford Circus, to name but a few. Changing at any of those stations will soon get you the short distance to Pimlico, just north of the River Thames.

There are a number of exits at Pimlico, but you want the main one on the corner of Redmayne Street and Bessborough Street. When you emerge you want to be opposite a sign on the wall saying Redmayne Street. There is a helpful map on a pillar just outside the main entrance, so you should be able to navigate yourself in the right direction.

A number of roads converge here, and you'll need to find the one called Tachbrook Street, which is directly opposite the main entrance. Now all you have to do is walk down Tachbrook Street, crossing Moreton Street along the way, and the pub is on the corner of Charlwood Street underneath some brown brick flats.

LOCAL INFORMATION

When you leave Pimlico tube station you're closer to the Thames than you are to the pub, so you might want to take the short stroll to the river and see if you can find the Thames Path, which pops up in several places around here. It's always pleasant to take a look at life on the river.

You're also not too far away from Victoria, with all the hustle and bustle of activity that always seems to be taking place around there.

The pub is only about a ten-minute walk from Westminster Cathedral, if you carry on along Tachbrook Street until you hit Vauxhall Bridge Road, then cross over and turn almost immediately right into Francis Street. It dates back to the end of the 19th century, and until just 11 years before the foundation stone was laid for the cathedral, it was the site of a prison. The interior is stunning, soaring high above you, and there is – of course – a gift shop if you want to add to your collection of London souvenirs.

> 6 Charlwood St, London SW1V 2EE
> Open: Mon-Sat noon-11pm, Sun noon-10.30pm
> Food: Mon-Fri noon-3pm and 5pm-10pm, Sat-Sun 12.30pm-9.30pm
> Tel: 020 763 7225
> www.caskpubandkitchen.com

DESCRIPTION

CASK Pub & Kitchen may be just outside the very heart of the city, but it's one of the top pubs to visit if you like a decent selection of beer to choose from.

Beer festivals are frequent (there was a Yorkshire one on when we were in one time), though it can feel like every day is a beer festival. There are 10 cask ales on permanently, and thanks to their website's handy 'Today's Beer List' button you can prepare in advance. At the moment we can see that they have Dissolution IPA from Kirkstall on, which is delicious, although we wouldn't mind sampling the Oatmeal Stout from St Andrew's Brew Co. There are also 15 keg lines to try, and the fridges are stocked with enough bottles to keep you busy for a long, long time.

Although there was something of a refurbishment to mark the pub's 5th birthday in 2014, it maintained the large open feel pretty well, even if it could do with a few more chairs as it can get very busy. Don't expect a typical old school boozer. This is very much a modern drinking venue with a relaxing feel to the fixtures and fittings, and a slightly more formal area suited to dining off to one side. There is also an overspill area outside with some benches and tables, if the weather's up to it.

THE DOVE

Photo courtesy of The Dove

HOW TO GET THERE

First step of the journey is to get to Ravenscourt Park tube station, on the District line. Any westbound train that's displayed as Ealing Broadway or Richmond will do, just don't take one that says it's going to Wimbledon.

If you look at the walk from Ravenscourt Park to The Dove on Google Maps, it looks like a pretty straightforward one. Wrong. We want the Ravenscourt Road exit. Turn left on leaving the station, and walk until you reach a T-junction with King Street. Turn left here, and then almost immediately you'll have to cross the road and take a right down Rivercourt Road.

As you walk down Rivercourt Road you'll soon be aware of a dual carriageway in front of you. Turn left when you reach it and walk along until you reach a subway. Go down here, turn right to walk beneath the dual carriageway, and turn right again to head back to ground level and to be reunited with Rivercourt Road.

From here it's easy. Take a left down Rivercourt Road until you reach the River Thames and can go no further, then take a left to walk towards a narrow alleyway, and The Dove is on your right.

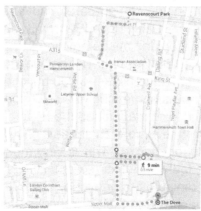

LOCAL INFORMATION

Like many pubs in the area, The Dove is owned by Fuller's Brewery. This is hardly surprising, as the brewery is only a quarter of an hour's walk from the pub. The brewery first opened in the 19th century, with Fuller's Smith and Turner coming into being in 1845, and one of their beers is named after that year. The brewery has been on the same site ever since, and you can book a tour of it and get to know a lot more about the history of the brewery and its beers.

If you're lucky, The Mawson Arms pub will be open. It's on the brewery site, and if you go in do try a pint of ESB. We've never had a better pint of it than in this pub. The pub has two names, you can see a pub sign for The Mawson Arms and one for The Fox and Hounds. Nobody seems quite sure why it has two names, although there are plenty of theories.

And if you think Fuller's just brew beer and run pubs, then go and visit their brewery shop. We were amazed at the range of products when we walked in for the first time.

First Floor, Paddington Station, London W2 1HB
Open: Mon-Sat 8am-11pm, Sun 10am-10.30pm
Food: Mon-Sat 8am-9.30pm, Sun 10am-9.30pm
Tel: 020 7402 2441
www.madbishopandbear.co.uk

DESCRIPTION

If we had to spend the rest of our days only visiting one pub in London, The Dove would be it. When you step through the front doorway, it's like being transported back in time. Old, dark wood, a mixture of tiled and wooden floor, exposed brickwork, it all catches the eye.

There's a compact bar area in front of the door, and a step or two takes you up to another level, commonly used by people dining here. Beyond that you come to an outdoor seating area that overlooks the River Thames and offers marvellous views of the Thames flowing by.

The pub has been around since the 17th century, and how many pubs can lay claim to receiving King Charles II as he courted his mistress Nell Gwynne? That was in 1668. There are frames on the walls that detail some of the people who have drunk here, and if it's good enough for Ernest Hemingway it's good enough for us. The name we were most pleased to see was that of James Thomson, who was inspired to write the poem 'Rule Britannia' whilst relaxing here. Later set to music by Thomas Arne in 1740, it is now known around the world. It made us feel very patriotic.

THE LAMB

HOW TO GET THERE

Russell Square is the nearest tube station to The Lamb, and it's on the Piccadilly line. This means it's just a short distance from the likes of King's Cross, Holborn, Covent Garden or Leicester Square.

When you step into daylight you'll find yourself on Bernard Street. Take a right turn, and carry on walking until you go past the pleasant Brunswick Square Gardens. When you reach the end of the gardens, turn right (not that you've got much choice) until you reach a T-Junction with Guilford Street. Turn left here, until you see Guilford Place on your right. Turn into Guildford Place, which soon becomes Lamb's Conduit Street, and the pub will appear on your left.

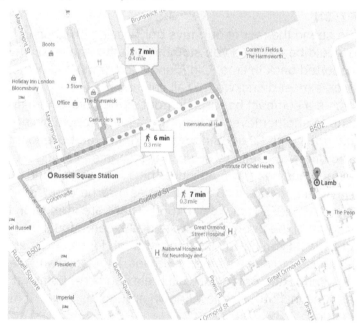

LOCAL INFORMATION

If you'd turned left out of Russell Street Station and then taken a left down Herbrand Street, you would have found yourself confronted with something called The Horse Hospital. This no longer has anything to do with horses, being a converted stable, but is now something that describes itself as 'providing space for underground and avant-garde media since 1993'. So that clears that one up.

Russell Square, from which the station takes its name, can be found by turning left out of the tube station and keeping going for a few minutes until you reach the Square.

The Charles Dickens Museum (he's here again) isn't too far away, and you can find it by ignoring the turning down Guilford Place and carrying on along Guilford Street until you reach Doughty Street on your right. Number 48 is the place that you're looking for, and it's a former home of the great man himself. The British Museum is also in the area, near Russell Square, and we can't recommend it highly enough.

6 Charlwood St, London SW1V 2EE
Open: Mon-Sat noon-11pm, Sun noon-10.30pm
Food: Mon-Fri noon-3pm and 5pm-10pm, Sat-Sun 12.30pm-9.30pm
Tel: 020 763 7225
www.caskpubandkitchen.com

DESCRIPTION

The Lamb, despite the woolly creature on the pub sign, is not named after an animal normally found on farms. Instead, it is named after William Lambe, the man responsible for the funding of the Conduit from which the street takes its name. In 1564 he donated £1,500 to cover the rebuilding of the Conduit, a considerable sum in its day. This would carry the area's plentiful supply of water to places that needed it. In addition to the usual range of beers from Young's you'll usually find a few guests on, so you should always find something to your satisfaction.

Inside this quirky Grade II listed gem from the 1720s, much praise is rightly lavished on the etched snob screens above the bar in certain areas, so that the upper classes didn't have to gaze on us commoners, while the images of Victorian actresses on the walls command slightly less attention. Well worth a look, all the same, as are the rest of the decorations.

Our favourite item is the working polyphon, which can be played in aid of charity. It's what came before the gramophone player, and if that term doesn't mean anything to you, then it's what came before the iPod and the mobile phone. Speaking of which, there's no television in the pub and, bar the polyphon, no music either. Bliss.

THE BUCKINGHAM ARMS

HOW TO GET THERE

The nearest station to the Buckingham Arms is St. James's Park, on the Circle (yellow) and District (green) lines. On leaving the station you want the Broadway exit, which should see you reach daylight with a roundabout in front of you and a pub called The Old Star on the opposite side of the road.

Turn immediately left when you step onto the pavement in front of the station, without crossing over towards the Old Star, and walk along a road that is now called Petty France. You'll soon reach a turning on the left called Palmer Street and a pub called The Adam and Eve on the corner of Palmer Street and Petty France, but all you have to do is keep on along Petty France and ignore any turnings to left or right.

Passing by The Adam and Eve, and still on Petty France, the next turning on the left is a little alleyway called Vandon Passage. Go straight across the road, leaving the alleyway behind you, and The Buckingham will very shortly appear on your left hand side.

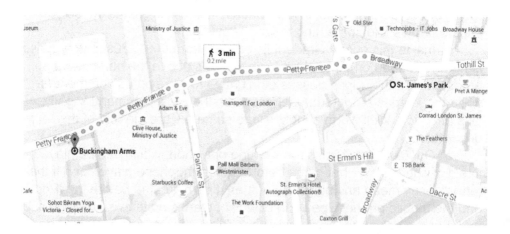

LOCAL INFORMATION

In your haste to get to the pub, you may not have noticed walking past a large office block housing the Ministry Of Justice. Well, it hardly advertises itself with big neon signs. They've only been here on this site since 2008, but the street itself is much older. Back in the 15th century, when Westminster would have been a mainly green and pleasant land, French wool merchants decided the best way to facilitate trade with London was to go and live there. They all congregated together, and there were so many of them that locals complained about not hearing a word of English. The street's still named Petty France.

You're also very close to St. James's Park. If you've time for a detour, turn right and cross the road when you reach Palmer Street and keep going along that street. The park will soon be in front of you. At this point you could turn left and walk the short distance along Birdcage Walk towards Buckingham Palace.

Birdcage Walk was where the Royal Aviary used to be, having first established itself under James I in the early 17th century. It's where the royal hunting birds used to be housed.

62 Petty France, London SW1H 9EU
Open: Mon-Fri 11am-11pm, Sat-Sun 11am-6pm
Food: Mon-Fri noon-5pm, Sat-Sun noon-9pm
Tel: 020 7222 3386
www.youngs.co.uk/pubs/buckingham-arms

DESCRIPTION

The Buckingham Arms makes the most of its royal location near the palace from which it takes its name, and why not? It only acquired the Buckingham name in 1901, having been known as the Black Horse from its first appearance in the late 18th century. There have been several refurbishments since then, the one that started in 1898 saw it morph into the Buckingham Arms, and a tasteful renovation in the early part of the current century saw many of the original features retained.

These include the etched mirrors behind the bar, which curves around majestically, and they even added some stained glass screens. These, together with a fine collection of royalty-themed artwork adorning the walls, and the fine leaded windows, make an attractive setting for a leisurely drink.

The pub is quite spacious and open, and seemed relatively quiet on a recent Friday night visit. On the plus side, it did make it easy to find a stool and rest our pints on a convenient shelf. The pub is part of the Young's family, and thus supplies their traditional run of ales, but guest beers also appear. We had a Phoenix Smoked Porter from the Wimbledon Brewery last time we were there. Lightly smoked and very smooth, it was delicious.

THE VIADUCT TAVERN

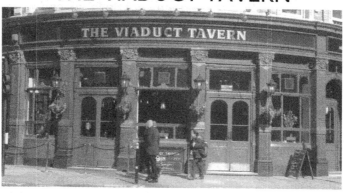

HOW TO GET THERE

St. Paul's is the closest underground stop to The Viaduct Tavern, and for that you'll need to travel on the Central line (red one). Liverpool Street to the east and Tottenham Court Road to the west make good connecting points on the Central line.

Look for Exit 2 and make your way up to Newgate Street. You remain on Newgate Street all the way to the pub, taking care to take the left fork when the road splits in two shortly after leaving the tube station. Taking the right one will lead you up King Edward Street, where after a short walk some people may be delighted to find a turning off to the right called Little Britain (first turning on the right after Angel Street, if you want to take any pictures of a Little Britain street sign).

Back on Newgate Street, just make your way along here until you get to the junction with Giltspur Street on the right, and the pub will be next to you.

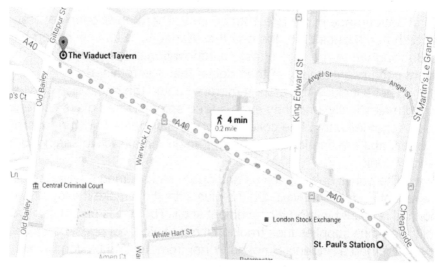

LOCAL INFORMATION

As we're so close to the Old Bailey, it would be a shame not to have a look at it, as it will only take you a few minutes to get there from The Viaduct Tavern. Better to look at it from the outside as a free person, than from the inside as a prisoner.

The Old Bailey, or more properly the Central Criminal Court (it's on a street called Old Bailey, hence the name), dates back to 1902 in its present form, although trials have been held here since the end of the 16th century. They were still hanging people in the street in 1868!

If gazing from the outside isn't enough for you, there is free access to the public galleries, but with only limited admission times and some pretty strict rules. No under 14s, for instance, and absolutely no electronic items, bags, food or drink are allowed. And no, you can't leave items at reception to be picked up later. Despite all these understandably draconian measures, the Old Bailey can still become very busy inside, so let's head back up Old Bailey street and find The Viaduct Tavern.

126 Newgate St, London EC1A 7AA
Open: Mon-Fri 8.30am-11pm, Sat-Sun closed
Food: Mon-Fri noon-8pm
Tel: 020 7600 1863
www.viaducttavern.co.uk

DESCRIPTION

The pub is a fine old building from the outside, but inside it switches to a higher plane altogether. It's a genuine survivor of the Victorian gin-palace days, which can be seen in virtually every corner of the pub. Plenty of beer, though, because it's a Fuller's house, so no worries on that score.

Dating from 1869, the pub still features an old booth from which the landlady would dispense gin tokens to customers which they could later swap at the bar for more gin (not everybody was trusted to handle money in those days). In a way there's almost too much history here to take in with just one visit. For instance, it is alleged that the old Newgate Prison cells were down in what is now the basement of the pub, harking back to an era when some criminals would be publicly executed.

The pub has a magnificent interior, with ornate mirrors, decorative glasswork, and large wall murals depicting various different themes e.g. banking, or the arts. Don't forget to look up at the ceiling, either, with its interlocking swirling panels, and make a special point of going to the back of the pub to see the etched glass panels alongside the old gin booth. Lovers of gin will be in heaven. Beer lovers like us will feel pretty content as well.

THE DEFECTOR'S WELD

Photo courtesy of The Defector's Weld

HOW TO GET THERE

Although The Defector's Weld is only a short walk from BrewDog Shepherd's Bush, a bar covered elsewhere in this book, the nearest underground station is different. It's Shepherd's Bush Market, on the Hammersmith and City line (the pink one), as well as a branch of the Circle line (yellow).

Shepherd's Bush Market is one stop from Goldhawk Road (the nearest one to BrewDog), and if you want to walk from one bar to the other, BrewDog is at the bottom left corner of Shepherd's Bush Green (or south west, if you prefer) and The Defector's Weld is at the top left corner (or north west). Just walk along by the side of the green and you'll soon get from one to the other.

On leaving the station at Shepherd's Bush Market you will find yourself on Uxbridge Road. Turn left, and after a two-minute walk you'll see The Defector's Weld in front of you and on the other side of the road. Make good use of the traffic lights as it gets very busy around here.

LOCAL INFORMATION

The origin behind the pub's name is obscure, although the 'Defector' part is thought to refer to a spy during the Cold War, one of a ring of spies from Cambridge who worked for the BBC just up the road at White City. We've seen various theories for the 'Weld' section of the name, but it's anybody's guess, really. Perhaps it's because the British spies joined together to pass information on to Russia, so the defectors welded together. Who knows? What we do know is that these days we have a very fine pub with lots of beers from local breweries, so let's pay it a visit.

170 Uxbridge Road, London W12 8AA
Open: Mon-Thu noon-midnight, Fri-Sat noon-2am (no admission after midnight), Sun noon-11pm
Food: Daily noon-10pm
Tel: 020 8749 0008
www.defectors-weld.co.uk

DESCRIPTION

Rather surprisingly, given the extended range of beers on display, The Defector's Weld is part of the Young's brewery empire (we know, it's Charles Wells these days). You don't normally find breweries like Signature Brew, Beavertown and Camden Town in a Young's pub, but they're common here. When Young's bought it in 2014 they wisely did nothing to it apart from a modest refurbishment, and left the pub doing what it does best: serving beer and food.

Our notes from the last trip tell us that it takes four minutes to get here from BrewDog, and that it was fairly quiet on a Thursday lunchtime, although getting very busy in the evening on subsequent visits. Most people occupy the large horseshoe-shaped bar downstairs, which is where we spent most of our time apart from a brief spell of being nosy and wandering around the entire pub.

It's a comfortable place, spacious, renovated in a pleasing way, and it's what can only be described as 'a London boozer'. We occupied stools at the bar on a recent visit, and chatted away to a young woman behind the bar who clearly knew her beer, as we were expertly guided towards various different ales. We love places like this, and we hope they survive for a long time to come.

THE KINGS ARMS

HOW TO GET THERE

For The Kings Arms you want Southwark station, which is only on the Jubilee line. Leaving the station gives you a bewildering choice of four streets, and they all look like they're busy and important. Try to spot a large pub on the other side of the road called The Ring, but don't cross over to it, it's just a direction finder. Face the pub, and The Cut is the road leading off to your right. You want the road heading to your left, which is called Blackfriars Road.

Walk off to the left, then, without crossing the road, and you'll soon be strolling underneath a railway bridge. Keep going, and in a moment or two you'll arrive at Meymott Street on your left. Turn into Meymott Street, and keep on it until you reach a junction with Hatfields. Roupell Street is almost immediately opposite you, so cross over and go down Roupell Street.

From here it won't be long before you reach the Kings Arms, which is on the corner of Roupell Street and Windmill Walk.

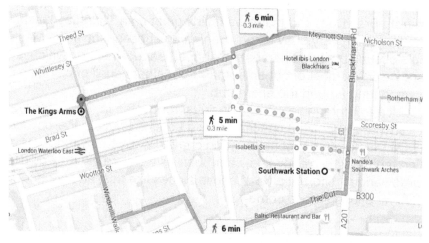

LOCAL INFORMATION

Although parts of it are very old, the Jubilee line is the youngest of all the lines on the London underground network. It was named in honour of the Silver Jubilee of Queen Elizabeth II, which was in 1977, although the line only formally opened in 1979.

It was originally going to be called The Fleet Line, after London's underground river, but 25 years of Queen Elizabeth's reign saw to that. It is mainly cobbled together from bits of other lines that used to run under different names in the past, although an extension completed in 1999 took it all the way from Green Park out to Stratford.

Nowadays it would take you an hour to travel from one end of the Jubilee Line (Stanmore) to the other (Stratford), but you only need to get to Southwark, so let's go there and stroll to the pub. Reflect, as you get near, that in the 19th century the street on which the pub stands largely consisted of workers' cottages.

25 Roupell St, London SE1 8TB
Open: Mon-Sat 11am-11pm, Sun noon-10.30pm
Food: Mon-Fri 11.30am-10.30pm, Sat 1pm-10.30pm, Sun noon till they run out!
Tel: 020 7207 0784
http://thekingsarmslondon.co.uk

DESCRIPTION

Make no mistake about it, this is a big pub. It seems to keep on expanding as you walk through it, until you end up in a dining area that makes you feel like you've somehow stumbled into a farmhouse. It certainly belies the rather dour exterior (it has been an undertakers in the past).

Inside, though, it's a lot more cheerful, and this Georgian pub serves up a pleasant surprise in that the farmhouse at the back is actually a Thai restaurant. As always, be aware that it can get very busy a lot of the time, especially when five o'clock comes around and everybody streams out of the office. We found a spot roughly in the middle of the pub, put our pints down on a convenient shelf nearby, and watched the world go by. Even when it's packed, it doesn't seem to cater for one particular category of people. Locals, tourists, workers - all happily co-mingle, and there's a pleasing mix of suits and casuals.

Plenty of prints decorate the walls, and various interesting curios are dotted about the place. We spotted a scooter on one stroll through, which may have belonged to a customer, although it looked a lot more permanent than that. As for the beer, there are usually ten or so pumps to choose from, and Dark Star appears to be a recurring favourite, which always does the job for us.

THE WHITE HART BREW PUB

HOW TO GET THERE

Stepney Green is the best tube station for The White Hart Brew Pub at the moment, and it's served by the District (green) and Hammersmith and City (pink) lines. Whitechapel tube station is closer than Stepney Green by a couple of minutes, but owing to its part in the CrossRail development, the whereabouts of the entrances and exits are subject to change, and may disappear altogether.

Although the District line has several branch lines in the western part of London, the eastern section of it is just one line, so you can get on to any train going eastbound in the confident knowledge that you'll get to Stepney Green.

There's only the one exit from Stepney Green station, and this will place you on Mile End Road. Turn right when you leave the station, and basically it's a case of keep on going and the White Hart Brew Pub will turn up within a few minutes. As markers along the way, you'll go past Cephas Avenue on your right, along with Cleveland Way, Bardsey Place and then a little chunk of Edward Passage Road before the pub is there on your right.

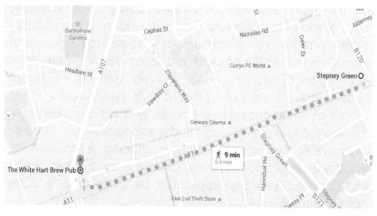

LOCAL INFORMATION

Preparing a book like this takes a lot of planning. There were over 90 pubs on the final shortlist, some of which had been known personally for over 40 years (take a bow, The Lamb on Lamb's Conduit Street, The Princess Louise, The Ship and Shovell, The Flask and The Holly Bush), so it's a joy when a pub springs up out of nowhere and immediately catapults itself into the book. The White Hart Brew Pub is one such place.

Stepney Green was being visited so that a renowned nearby pub could come under scrutiny, but alas it fell short. There was only a handful of beers on offer and, as we were being served, a large ginger cat walked along the top of the bar between us and the chap pulling the pint. The cat ignored all hygiene rules and strode regally onwards. The pint was fairly ordinary, and we left the pub feeling somewhat deflated as we turned to walk back to Stepney Green tube station. Then out of curiosity we crossed over the road, and saw the White Hart Brew Pub.

1 Mile End Road, London E1 4TP
Open: Daily 10.30am-midnight
Food: Mon-Fri noon-3pm and 6pm-10pm, Sat 10.30am-10pm, Sun 10.30am-9pm
Tel: 020 7790 2894
www.the-white-hart.co.uk/home

DESCRIPTION

The first thing you notice on entering this capacious East End Victorian boozer is that it's furnishings are, to be polite, eclectic. It's functional, it works (there's an excellent glass partition), it's all smart and new following a recent refurbishment, but it looks like it has been obtained from half a dozen different sources. Nonetheless, it has a certain charm, and we can forgive anything about a pub that has a micro-brewery in the basement.

The brewery goes by the name of One Mile End, and you can be sure of spotting one or more of their beers on the bar. However, on a recent visit we saw a porter from the Celt Experience brewery called Dark Age, and plumped for that instead. It was splendid stuff, just what a porter should be like, and we doff our non-existent hats to them.

It certainly lifted the spirits after the experience of the cat at the other pub. Don't get us wrong, we love cats, we just don't think that they should be walking along the top of a bar when beer is being served.

There's a mixed clientele, always a good sign, and it's a combination of locals and visitors alike. We felt at home, sipping our pints of porter, and there's no finer recommendation for a pub than that.

THE KING'S HEAD

Photo courtesy of The King's Head

HOW TO GET THERE

The King's Head is down at the southern end of the Northern line, and your nearest tube station is Tooting Bec. Bear in mind when buying your ticket that it's in Zone 3 of the tube network. As with all stations in this part of London, you might have to change tube trains at Kennington to get one going as far as Morden.

Incidentally, your journey will take you through Balham, which older readers will remember Peter Sellers describing as the 'Gateway to the South.' Younger readers can find it on YouTube: https://youtu.be/8RTWk9QIKS0.

Regardless of which exit you take out of the tube station, you'll see a pub called The Wheatsheaf on the opposite side of the road. The pub stands on the corner of Trinity Road and Upper Tooting Road, and it is the latter that you'll need to walk down to get to the King's Head. If you find yourself on Balham High Road, turn through 180 degrees and reverse direction to get back to Upper Tooting Road.

After passing several streets with interesting names on your right (Noyna, Fircroft, Mandrake and Beechcroft), you'll find the pub set back from the road on the right.

LOCAL INFORMATION

The 'Bec' part of the name comes from Bec Abbey in Normandy, as it was given land in this part of London after the Norman Conquest. Eventually we got it back, but the Bec part remains.

It's hard to believe, as you saunter along Upper Tooting Road, that Tooting Bec was mentioned in the Domesday Book way back in 1086. There probably wasn't much to it then, and to be honest, the pub's about the most interesting thing that you'll find here.

However, it's worth mentioning that on nearby Tooting Bec Road you'll find The Lido, which the local council describes as 'the largest, fresh water, open air swimming pool in England'. If you fancy a dip, you should check the opening hours on their website, as they vary throughout the year: www.placesforpeopleleisure.org/centres/tooting-bec-lido.

> 84 Upper Tooting Rd, London SW17 7PB
> Open: Mon-Thu noon-midnight, Fri-Sat noon-1am,
> Sun noon-11pm
> Tel: 020 8767 6708
> http://kingsheadpub-tooting.co.uk

DESCRIPTION

Stand outside the pub and have a good look at it before you go in, because it's a lovely old building. The inside's none too shabby either. The pub was rebuilt in 1897, although a pub has existed on the site since the end of the 18th century. The image on the pub sign is that of King Henry VIII, but even this marvellous place cannot claim to be that old.

It's a Taylor Walker pub, and there were over half a dozen ales on offer at the bar when we last went in. Purists may turn up their noses at Old Speckled Hen, but we rather enjoyed it. CAMRA (the UK's Campaign For Real Ale, for those not in the know) have described this as 'probably the most ornate pub in South London', and we can't argue with that. A fine refurbishment in 2015 did nothing to destroy the glass panelling, the extensive woodwork, the many tiles, and the bar fittings and various screens, which happily all survived intact.

There are some more modern furnishings, it's not all Victoriana, but they complement each other well, and help to disguise the fact that there are actually quite a few televisions in here. If you want to watch a game of football with your pint, there are few more attractive places to do it in.

THE ANTELOPE

Photo courtesy of The Antelope

HOW TO GET THERE

If you fancy tootling off to Tooting and visiting The Antelope, then Tooting Broadway is your nearest tube station, and you'll find it on the Northern line. This makes it easily reachable from the likes of Charing Cross, Euston Station and King's Cross. Just make sure that the tube is going as far as Morden, but even if the overhead information displays are saying that the next tube is only going as far as Kennington, you may as well catch it and change when you reach Kennington.

On arrival at Tooting Broadway, take a moment to examine the statue of King Edward VII that stands just outside the exit. If you can find anybody to tell you what it's doing there, good luck.

After staring at Edward for a while, and turning your back to the exit, you'll want to turn right on to Tooting High Street and almost immediately turn right again to walk down Mitcham Road. It will only be a few minutes before you go past Granada Street on your right, and keeping on Mitcham Road will bring you to The Antelope on the right in a matter of moments.

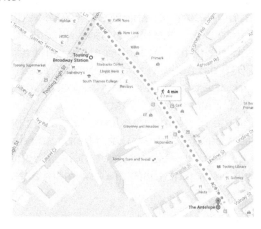

LOCAL INFORMATION

There are plenty of shops on Mitcham Road, but the most interesting place is, believe it or not, the Gala Bingo Club at 50 Mitcham Road. You might not think it when you look at it from outside, but we highly recommend you making a detour on your way to the pub, and stepping through the doors.

It used to be a cinema when it first opened in 1931, although it doubled up as a theatre and, briefly, hosted a circus. It had the distinction of being the first British cinema to be Grade I listed. One look inside will tell you why, and as many have said, it looks more like a palace than a bingo hall. Gala are to be commended for maintaining the building in such splendid style. After all, we are talking about a venue that has been host to the likes of The Rolling Stones, Frank Sinatra and The Beatles.

76 Mitcham Rd, London SW17 9NG
Open: Mon-Wed 4pm-11pm, Thu 4pm-midnight, Fri 4pm-1am,
Sat noon-1am, Sun noon-11pm
Food: Mon-Fri 5pm-10pm, Sat noon-4pm and 5pm-10pm,
Sun 12.30pm-7pm
Tel: 020 8672 3888
http://theantelopepub.com

DESCRIPTION

We've been in pubs with more stuffed animals on display, but not many. You'll be drinking your pint in the company of fox, deer and of course antelope.

There were around eight beers to choose from when we were last there, and we enjoyed a pint of Innovation, a lovely ruby red bitter. Beers travel from far and wide to get here, and we noted the likes of Adnams (Suffolk), Mallinsons (West Yorkshire) and Caledonian (Edinburgh). They also had two pumps of draught ciders.

The pub first opened in the 1800s, back in the day when Barclay referred to a brewery as well as a bank. The brewery in question (far more interesting than banking) was the Anchor Brewery, operated for a time by Mr Barclay and Mr Perkins. Once the biggest brewery in the world, it all came to a sad end in 1981 when the brewery building was demolished.

There's plenty of room inside The Antelope, with a rather grand dining room. At times it can seem a little bit too hip and trendy for its own good, but the range of beers more than compensates. And if it's a sunny day, there's always the beer garden to enjoy.

THE DOG AND DUCK

HOW TO GET THERE

Tottenham Court Road tube station is about a five-minute walk from The Dog and Duck, and the station is served by the Central and Northern lines. This gives you good access from Euston Station to the north and Charing Cross to the south (both Northern), and Oxford Circus to the west and Liverpool Street to the east (both Central).

When we last visited, getting to the pub was quite confusing because of the huge amount of roadworks going on. As you come out of the tube station you'll see a pub called The Flying Horse in front of you. Turn right and take a few steps to reach Charing Cross Road. The Dominion Theatre will be diagonally across the road from you. Turn right and start walking down Charing Cross Road.

Keep going till you see Manette Street on your right, just after Goslett Yard. Turn into it, walk until it comes to a T-junction, and turn left down Greek Street. The first street on your right will be Bateman Street, so turn into it and walk a short distance before the Dog and Duck turns up over the road at a crossroads.

LOCAL INFORMATION

The area around the tube station is very busy indeed. Back in the day, the Dominion Theatre used to be a cinema, and we remember going there to watch the first Star Wars film. Several of us students came out clutching our souvenir Star Wars straws and went into the nearest pub. We soon discovered that drinking beer through a straw is not a good idea. Don't try it.

Apart from old memories, there is a huge collection of shops around here, although unfortunately a lot of them are going be hidden for some considerable time while work goes ahead on the Cross Rail project to connect west and east London. If you want to take a slightly less stressful walk to the pub away from all the roadworks, turn left out of the tube station and walk along Oxford Street until you see Soho Street on your left. Walk for a little way until you reach Soho Gardens, and walk directly across the middle of them, or at least make sure that you leave them on the opposite side from where you entered. On leaving, turn right onto Soho Square and almost immediately left onto Frith Street and carry on until the pub comes into view on the right.

18 Bateman St, London W1D 3AJ
Open: Daily 10am-11pm
Tel: 020 7494 0697
www.nicholsonspubs.co.uk/restaurants/london/
thedoganddducksoholondon

DESCRIPTION

The Dog and Duck is a Nicholson's pub, and if you're familiar with their extensive chain then you'll have some idea of what to expect. The present pub was built in 1897, and is a fine example of the architecture of the time. Glazed tiles were obviously all the rage then, because there are literally thousands of them decorating the place, alongside several ornate mirrors. It really is a lovely building, but it can get very busy on occasions, as it was when we were there on a Saturday lunchtime.

If it is getting too packed and you're here for some food, the upstairs dining room is usually quieter, and is a decent place to escape to. It's wise to book in advance. Madonna must have thought it was a lovely pub as well, because she's been served here, as – on more than one occasion – was George Orwell.

Being a good Nicholson's pub, there's quite a range of beers to choose from, and our pints of Honey Porter from Milestone Brewery were in good form. For once you could actually taste the honey, and there was a fair amount of chocolate in it as well. Winnie the Pooh would have approved. Perhaps it should be re-named 'Winnie the Brew'.

THE MUSEUM TAVERN

HOW TO GET THERE

There are a couple of tube stations you could take for The Museum Tavern, namely Tottenham Court Road and Holborn. We've opted for Tottenham Court Road as it's a couple of minutes closer. These things matter when you're thirsty.

Tottenham Court Road is on the Central and Northern lines. Due to the vast amount of roadworks going on in the area thanks to the Cross Rail development, there is only one exit at the time of writing. If you're lucky enough to find more than one exit open, take the one for Oxford Street.

On reaching Oxford Street there should be a pub in front of you called The Flying Horse, which till recently was called The Tottenham, but before that it was the Flying Horse originally. And there's a whole other story behind that pub too, the only historic pub you'll find on all of Oxford Street!

A few yards to the right as you face The Flying Horse is Tottenham Court Road, going north. Walk up here a few yards and cross to the far side at the pedestrian crossing. Turn left and carry on up Tottenham Court Road, then take the first street on the right. This is Great Russell Street and it will lead you to The Museum Tavern, on your right.

LOCAL INFORMATION

As the name implies, this pub is close to a museum. In fact, as you stand in front of the pub with your back to it and gaze to the north across Great Russell Street, you'll get a splendid view of The British Museum.

It's a good spot for a pub. If you do visit the museum, by the time you come out you'll be in need of a drink and a spot of quiet relaxation while you recover from the sensory overload that you've just experienced.

There are other museums in the area, although nothing on quite the same scale. The Cartoon Museum is on Little Russell Street just one minute's walk away by strolling down Coptic Street and turning left. And if you ever wanted to see the stuffed bear from British comedy classic Steptoe and Son, The Museum of Comedy is just around the corner on Bloomsbury Way. Needless to say, there's a lot more to look at than a stuffed bear.

49 Great Russell St, London WC1B 3BA
Open: Mon-Thu 11am-11.30pm, Fri-Sat 11am-midnight, Sun 10am-10pm
Food: Mon-Sat 11am-11pm, Sun noon-9pm
Tel: 020 7242 8987
www.taylor-walker.co.uk/pub/museum-tavern-bloomsbury/c0747

DESCRIPTION

The pub is part of the Taylor Walker group and has a long history, dating back to the early 18th century when there was a pub on the site called The Dog and Duck, hinting at the hunting that used to take place on the nearby marshland. When The British Museum opened up in the 1760s, the pub opportunistically changed its name to The Museum Tavern.

The current building can trace a lot of its fixtures and fittings back to 1855, although they've lost some things along the way, like the partitions that used to give Victorian drinkers their much-loved privacy. However, plenty still remains, and you'll find much elaborate wood and glasswork to entertain the eye.

Quite a few beers were on when we last went, and we had a rather pleasant honey mild. Little did we know that honey beers were clearly the in thing at the time, because a few more popped up on the same day in various different pubs.

When you're having your drink, reflect on the fact that the likes of Karl Marx and Sir Arthur Conan Doyle used to drink here. We wonder if any Sherlock Holmes stories were plotted in The Museum Tavern?

THE JUNCTION TAVERN

HOW TO GET THERE

Although The Junction Tavern is only a short walk away from Tufnell Park tube station, there is a great danger of setting off in the wrong direction if you're visiting here for the first time, especially if it's dark. Tufnell Park is on the High Barnet branch of the Northern line, so the usual rule about changing at Camden Town applies if every display above the platform is stubbornly stuck on tubes going to Edgware.

There are two exits at Tufnell Park, and you want to take the one that will bring you out on to Brecknock Road, opposite a bar called Aces and Eights. As there are five roads to choose from after leaving the station, please make sure you're on the right one!

Cross over towards Aces and Eights, ignoring it completely, and turn right to go past the front door and then walk around it to the left. This will bring you on to Fortess Road, and from here it's easy. You'll only be on Fortess Road for a couple of minutes before Lady Somerset Road turns up on the right, and The Junction Tavern is on the corner where the two roads meet up.

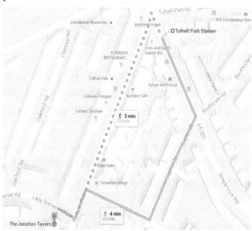

LOCAL INFORMATION

Lady Somerset Road is one of quite a few roads in this area of London that owe their name to St. John's College in Cambridge. St. John's used to own a large estate hereabouts, and the nearby Lady Margaret Road is named after the woman who started the work that eventually led to the foundation of St. John's. She was King Henry VIII's paternal grandmother, so we're not exactly talking recent history.

Never to be outdone by their great rivals, Oxford is also on the scene in the form of Christ Church College, which still owns the freehold on numerous roads in the vicinity.

Two other pubs in this book are not too far off, namely The Southampton Arms and The Pineapple, and whilst doing some research for this book we enjoyed a very pleasant Sunday lunchtime visiting all three. The order in which you visit them is entirely up to you, of course, but if you're starting at The Pineapple and then going to The Southampton Arms before ending up at The Junction Tavern, we'd stick to main roads between the first two of those pubs, even if it does mean a little backtracking. We tried a shortcut, with the usual result that we ended up taking twice as long as if we'd stayed on the streets.

101 Fortess Road, London NW5 1AG
Open: Mon-Thu 5pm-11pm, Fri-Sat noon-midnight,
Sun noon-11pm
Tel: 020 7485 9400
www.junctiontavern.co.uk

DESCRIPTION

This Victorian pub can date itself back to 1885, and although there's not much sign of that from the outside, there's plenty of evidence of its Victorian roots when you open the door and step inside.

The side of the pub that faces Fortess Road houses the dining area, which is quite open and welcoming, while the drinkers amongst us will gravitate naturally to the back of the pub and the more dedicated bar area. Here you'll find plenty of large mirrors and wood panelling, with complementary panelling around the decorative bar. If all that isn't enough for you, there's also a conservatory and a fine beer garden.

It's a free house, and always has a number of local ales on, but others can appear as well. On one of our visits, Otter's Amber made for a good session ale, golden colour, a little bit bitter, and with an interesting toffee undertone to it.

One note of warning: if you're coming here for a meal, you'd be advised to book in advance. If you're merely coming here for a drink, just turn up, head to the bar, and enjoy the beer.

THE GEORGE IV

Photo courtesy of The George IV

HOW TO GET THERE

Turnham Green underground station is our nearest stop, and it's served by both the District and the Piccadilly lines, giving a choice of routes. If you're using the District line, it doesn't matter whether the tube is going to Ealing Broadway or Richmond, because Turnham Green is the last stop before the line divides into two. However, treat the Piccadilly line with caution, as currently the majority of tube trains don't stop at Turnham Green. We'd advise you to change at Hammersmith and catch a District line service instead.

On leaving the station by its only exit, turn left and start walking down Turnham Green Terrace. There are some interesting shops around here, and even though one called Trotters is nothing to do with Only Fools and Horses and the adventures of Del-Boy and Rodney (it's a children's clothes shop), it still made us smile. And why anyone would think of calling a women's clothes shop Sweaty Betty is quite beyond us.

Keep going until you reach Chiswick High Road, at which point you turn right. Cross over by the traffic lights that are a few steps away, and turn right. Keep walking along the High Road and the George IV will soon appear on the left.

LOCAL INFORMATION

They really do have a thing for shop names around here. You'll probably notice American Pie (clothes shop), Churchill's (a pharmacy), Chiswick Cobblers (which is a shoe repair shop, not an insult) and many more.

There are plenty of dining options in the area too, although the pub itself is no slouch when it comes to providing food. The pub is on a single lane stretch of road separated from Chiswick High Road, and is remarkably well served. There's even a bank at one end of the road and a police station at the other end. Just about everything is catered for in this short stretch of road.

One practical point: we have Turnham Green tube station down as the nearest, which indeed it is, but The George IV is only a 10-minute walk from The Old Pack Horse, which is mentioned elsewhere in this book. Chiswick High Road conveniently connects the two pubs.

185 Chiswick High Rd, London W4 2DR
Open: Sun-Thu noon-11pm, Fri-Sat noon-1am
Food: Mon-Fri noon-3pm and 5pm-10pm, Sat noon-10pm,
Sun noon-8pm
Tel: 020 8994 4624
www.georgeiv.co.uk

DESCRIPTION

Before stepping into the pub, pause outside and take in its appearance. There was a fairly recent refurbishment, and they've done a very good job indeed. It doesn't take itself too seriously, though. When we were last there, a blackboard outside the pub cheerfully announced that it was 'London's Worst Quiz Night'. Two imposing pillars stand either side of the rather impressive front door, flanked by some large unadorned windows. The windows are sitting above two sets of tiles, and if you like tiles, just wait until you step inside.

The decoratively-panelled wooden bar dominates the main area of the pub, with a separate room at the back for comedy and music nights, and there's a sizeable beer garden area too. As if that wasn't enough, there's a games room upstairs. In the main bar there's a traditional pub theme, lots of wood and some open brick walls, a number of interesting prints on the walls, quite a collection of stuffed animals and, of course, beer.

The George IV is a Fuller's pub, so you can expect their range of beers. There usually appears to be a guest ale on, and we had the Oakham Citra when we were there one lunchtime. Some refurbishments can destroy the character of a pub, but this one stands as a fine example of how to get it right.

WATERLOO TAP

Photo courtesy of Waterloo Tap

HOW TO GET THERE

As its name implies, Waterloo Tap is not too far away from Waterloo underground station, and once you've been there a couple of times it's really very straightforward to find. However, first-time visitors can easily lose their way, as we did, so let's start from the underground station. This is on the Bakerloo, Jubilee, Northern (Charing Cross branch), and Waterloo and City lines. By way of a bit of tube trivia, Waterloo has 23 escalators, which is more than any other station.

The most straightforward approach when you get off the train, no matter which line you use, is to get yourself to the main station concourse and take stock. You'll now want to locate platform 18. From Platform 18, walk along past Starbucks and a small branch of Marks and Spencer, and take Exit 5 on the right (marked 'Way Out. Waterloo Bridge'). Go down a flight of steps to Station Approach. Nearly there!

Turn left on Station Approach, and in a short distance you'll come to a junction with York Road. Cross over at the convenient traffic lights that are slightly off to your right, and directly in front of you after crossing over you'll see Sutton Walk. Proceed along Sutton Walk, and Waterloo Tap will appear on the right-hand side tucked beneath a railway arch.

LOCAL INFORMATION

As you've probably guessed, Waterloo Station is named to honour Wellington's famous victory over Napoleon in 1815, although the battle actually took place not in Waterloo but just nearby. It saw the French under Napoleon taking on the combined might of forces from Britain, Germany, Belgium, Holland and Prussia. Waterloo was part of the United Kingdom of Netherlands at the time, but it now lies in Belgium.

When the Strand toll bridge across the Thames was rebuilt and re-opened in 1817 it was renamed Waterloo Bridge, also to celebrate Wellington's victory. Waterloo Station, originally called Waterloo Bridge Station, came along just over 30 years later, and finally changed its name to the current Waterloo Station in 1886.

There are several places and roads named after Waterloo in the area, but we're here for Waterloo Tap, so let's go and get a drink.

Arch 147, Sutton Walk, London SE1 7ND
Open: Mon-Wed noon-11pm, Thu-Fri noon-11.30pm, Sat 11am-11.30pm, Sun11am-10pm
Tel: 020 3455 7436
www.waterlootap.com

DESCRIPTION

This is the latest addition to a family of pubs that in London also includes Euston Tap, The Holborn Whippet, The Resting Hare and The Pelt Trader. They all have certain features in common, and most of them centre on beer. You won't find handpumps on the bar. Instead, you'll see a line or two of numerous dispensing fonts on a wall (brass is a favourite backdrop) behind the bar. In the case of Waterloo Tap, there are twenty keg lines and six cask lines on at any one time. Screens to either side of the bar area tell you what's currently available.

Don't be afraid that all the keg ones are going to be super-strength beers, because more often than not they won't be. Beavertown Brewery's Neck Oil, for example, a very sessionable IPA at 4.5%, went down a treat on a recent visit on what turned out to be a pretty warm day.

Waterloo Tap is business-like and functional in its décor, with lots of exposed brick overhead and practical tiles on the floor. It certainly won't win any awards as a Victorian gin palace restored to glory. It is pretty cool to be drinking under a railway arch, though, and there'll be more than one train missed from lingering at Waterloo Tap.

THE UNION TAVERN

HOW TO GET THERE

The nearest underground station to The Union Tavern is Westbourne Park, which lies on the Hammersmith and City line, as well as being on a branch of the Circle line. In keeping with one or two other pubs in this part of London, you're advised to stick to the Hammersmith and City line.

Two nearby stops on the same line are Shepherd's Bush Market (The Defector's Weld is your nearest pub) and Goldhawk Road (BrewDog Shepherd's Bush), which gives you a nice run of three good pubs within half a dozen stops of each other. Carrying on further east along the line would take you to Paddington (The Mad Bishop and Bear) and Baker Street (The Barley Mow), giving you an even greater choice of destinations.

There are a couple of exits from Westbourne Park, and they will both place you on Great Western Road. Turn left, and head underneath the bridge in front of you. In a little while you'll see Elkstone Road on your left, but keep going along Great Western Road and you'll soon reach a bridge passing over the Grand Union Canal. The pub is immediately after the bridge and on your right.

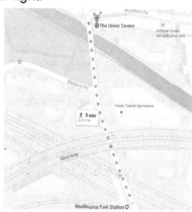

LOCAL INFORMATION

The Grand Union Canal is obviously the inspiration for the name of The Union Tavern, and it's the Paddington arm of the canal that you can see by the side of the pub. It stretches for about 140 miles from London to Birmingham, although if you take all of the branch lines into account it's closer to 286 miles.

Construction work began on the canal in 1793, and the original section of it took 12 years to complete. Now it's a collection of various different canals all joined together to form one lengthy waterway. Today there's very little by way of trade carried out on it, and its function is to serve the leisure industry.

On its way the canal could take you through the likes of Slough (well, something has to), Aylesbury, Northampton, Leicester and Oxford, before finally ending up in Birmingham. It would take around a week for a boat to get from one end to the other, and if you're feeling fit you can even walk the length of the canal towpath. We're going to the pub instead.

45 Woodfield Rd, London W9 2BA
Open: Mon-Thu noon-11pm, Fri-Sat noon-midnight, Sun noon-10.30pm
Food: Mon-Fri noon-4pm and 5pm-10pm, Sat noon-10pm, Sun noon-9pm
Tel: 020 7286 1886
www.union-tavern.co.uk

DESCRIPTION

On arriving at the pub, most people will grab a pint and wander outside to be on the terrace by the side of the canal, as there's an extensive outdoor seating area with a succession of large black umbrellas keeping the tables underneath them dry (usually) or out of the sun (rarely). Well, it's what we did anyway, and after finding our seats we just watched the canal's comings and goings while we sipped our pints.

This is a Fuller's pub so expect a good choice of their beers, but you will normally find several guest ales on sale as well, and the pub specialises in beers from other London breweries. We noted that there was a 'Meet the Brewer' night just five days after our last visit, which was to feature Weird Beard brewery from the splendidly named Trumpers Way in London W7.

The main bar is upstairs at street level, and is quite functional but comfortable, complete with wooden floor and a few food and drink photographs on the walls, along with some stools at the bar if you can manage to nab one. There's not too much in the way of decoration inside, although we did like the large Fuller, Smith and Turner mural on the wall outside above the main body of the pub. This is definitely a gastropub rather than a boozer.

THE RED LION

Photo courtesy of The Red Lion

HOW TO GET THERE

The nearest underground station to this splendid old Fuller's Brewery pub is Westminster, on the Circle (yellow), District (green) and Jubilee (grey) lines. Take Exit 4 and walk along Bridge Street away from the River Thames and with Big Ben and the Houses Of Parliament across the street. Google Maps bizarrely wants you to cross over to the other side of the road and then back again, but you can safely ignore that.

Go straight on when you reach Canon Row, with St. Stephen's Tavern in front of you. When you reach Parliament Street you turn right, where you'll see another underground entrance and exit! Yes, it is closer to The Red Lion than the exit described earlier, but you wouldn't have seen the Houses of Parliament if you'd used this exit, nor would you have been able to see the location of St. Stephen's Tavern. There's method in our madness. You can use the other exit next time for some unbridled excitement.

Proceed along Parliament Street for a little way until you reach a road called Derby Gate. Here you see The Red Lion in front of you, so simply cross over Derby Gate and in you go.

LOCAL INFORMATION

The Red Lion is the most popular pub name in Britain. One theory for this is that an order was issued by James VI of Scotland when he became James I of England in 1603. As a red lion featured on his coat of arms, he allegedly declared that all major buildings in England should bear a red lion. Undoubtedly some tavern owners responded as a sign of allegiance, but there is no record of this order being made.

Another theory concerns John of Gaunt, an immensely influential figure in the 14th century owing to his domination of the young King Richard II. Gaunt's crest featured a red lion, and while he wasn't well liked, it's thought that people displayed the red lion to show their disdain for Richard II. In retaliation, other pubs became The White Hart, the sign for Richard II. In addition, many local barons and landowners would have had a red lion on their crest, as it is a very popular heraldic figure, and publicans probably changed the name of their establishment in the hope of currying favour.

The truth is probably all of the above, depending on the pub. But that's enough talking about red lions. It's time to go and drink in one.

48 Parliament Street, London SW1A 2NH
Open: Mon-Fri 8am-11pm, Sat 8am-9pm, Sun 9am-9pm
Food: Mon-Fri 8am-11am and noon-10pm, Sat 8am-11am and noon-8pm, Sun 9am-11am and noon-7.30pm
Tel: 020 7930 5826
www.redlionwestminster.co.uk

DESCRIPTION

The Red Lion belongs to Fuller's Brewery, and there's been a pub or brewhouse on this site since 1434. The current pub is younger, having been rebuilt in the 1890s. It underwent a refurbishment in 2014, and can now be seen in all its Victorian grandeur, across three floors. The Cellar Bar has the distinctive air of a club, with some extremely comfortable seating in places (ordinary chairs and stools in others) and as befits the pub's Westminster location, plenty of political images around.

The main street level bar has another couple of collections of beer pumps, the majority from Fuller's. Decorative wood can be seen just about everywhere, and chandelier enthusiasts are in for a treat if they remember to look up at the ornate ceiling. Fine etched glass panels can be spotted here and there, and the scuffed wooden floor and the rather functional furnishings in this area tell you that this is very much a working pub. Being where it is, politicians and their helpers are often to be seen in here, and as in St. Stephen's Tavern nearby, don't be alarmed if a bell goes off. It's only calling the politicians back to vote, so as they all scarper out and have to get back across the road, you can relax and finish your drink at your leisure.

ST STEPHEN'S TAVERN

HOW TO GET THERE

The closest underground station to St. Stephen's Tavern is Westminster, which you can find on the Circle, District and Jubilee lines.

Getting to the pub from Westminster station couldn't be easier. Take the Bridge Street exit (Exit 4) and when you emerge you'll find yourself opposite the Houses of Parliament, with Big Ben standing proudly in front of you.

There's no need to cross the road, unless you're going sight-seeing. Turn right on leaving the station and walk till you reach a small side-street called Canon Row. This is often blocked off, but as long as you can cross over it you'll see the pub on the other side of the street.

We had a wonderful time with Google Maps, by the way. Although the route on the map below looks simple enough, it only works if you tell it you want to walk from the pub to the tube. That's why our little drinking man appears to be walking away from the pub, for once. If you reverse the directions, it sends you down to the Thames, across the road, walks you up to Parliament Street, back across the road, then back towards the tube station to get to the pub.

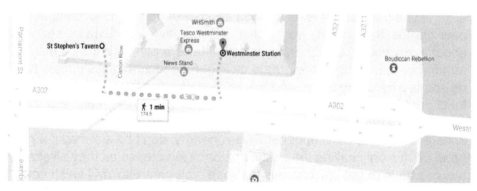

LOCAL INFORMATION

There are so many sights to see in this part of London that it's hard to know where to begin. We'll start with Big Ben. The name, as most people are aware, applies only to the Great Bell inside the tower, and not the tower itself. However, this 19th-century Gothic clock tower is almost always referred to as Big Ben. If you want a tour of it you'll have to be a UK resident and you'll need to ask your local MP very, very nicely. We highly recommend it, though, having been up there one time when the clock struck noon!

Tours of the Houses of Parliament are easier to book, and they'll take place on a Saturday unless Parliament is at recess, in which case they can take place on any day of the week. You should visit the parliament.uk/visiting website if you want to book them online.

Westminster Abbey is just around the corner from the Houses of Parliament, and it is absolutely magnificent. There's over one thousand years of history here, and anyone can turn up and visit it. If you decide to call in, be prepared to spend a few hours as there's an awful lot to see.

10 Bridge Street, London SW1A 2JR
Open: Mon-Sat 10am-11.30pm, Sun 10.30am-10.30pm
Food: Mon-Sat 10am-10pm, Sun 10.30am-10pm
Tel: 020 7925 2286
http://ststephenstavern.co.uk

DESCRIPTION

St. Stephen's Tavern is run by Badger Brewery. They've been around since 1777, which makes them around 100 years older than St. Stephen's Tavern itself. Not surprisingly, their beers feature prominently in the pub's offerings. It's a wonderfully ornate pub (don't forget to look up at the ceiling), with lots of political memorabilia. The wall by the side of the stairs up to a dining area is particularly well decorated with old newspaper cuttings, cartoons, portraits, photographs, all of a political slant.

Not surprisingly, as it's opposite the Houses of Parliament, various Members of Parliament do come in from time to time. The pub is so popular with MPs that it has its own Division Bell, and don't be alarmed if you hear it ringing. You'll be able to spot the MPs because they'll be the ones scurrying back across the road to cast their vote in the House.

No need for you to go anywhere, of course, you can just kick back and savour your drink in these fine surroundings. With so many attractions on its doorstep, St. Stephen's Tavern can get rather crowded on occasions, but you can always ring the Division Bell if it's getting too busy!

The Authors

Pete Gerrard went to London to study for a degree in astronomy at University College London, and in the finest student tradition perfected a 9-pub crawl through some of the city's finest pubs. He's been extending his London pub crawl ever since. Two of those original nine (The Lamb and The Princess Louise) are in this book.

Mike Gerrard is an award-winning travel and drinks writer, and a member of the British Guild of Beer Writers. He lived in London for 15 years, and has written about beer for magazines and websites including Beer Advocate, Perceptive Travel, The Huffington Post and the US drinks magazine Chilled, where he is an Editorial Staff Writer.

If you enjoyed this book and think it might be useful to other people, please take the time to go to Amazon and leave a positive review. It's appreciated by the publishers, and helpful to others. Thanks.

If you find any changes in the information, have any suggestions for improvements, or want to recommend a pub for possible future inclusion then email the publishers at **80Guides@gmail.com**. We're happy to listen to suggestions and hear about your discoveries.

And watch out for future titles from 80 Guides Publishing.

THE DOVE
Love the Dove
If you'd like to receive
treats, birthday offers
and news, join our
Mailing list today!

Made in United States
North Haven, CT
26 September 2022

24571964R00102